THESE ARE OUR BODIES

Talking Faith & Sexuality at Church & Home

Church Publishing
NEW YORK

LESLIE CHOPLIN AND JENNY BEAUMONT

Church Publishing Incorporated
19 East 34th Street, New York, NY 10016
www.churchpublishing.org

Cover design by Jennifer Kopec, 2 Pug Design
Typeset by Progressive Publishing Services

ISBN-13: 978-1-60674-308-9 (pbk.)
ISBN-13: 978-1-60674-309-6 (ebook)

Printed in the United States of America

CONTENTS

INTRODUCTION

In the past, society has viewed sex as a taboo subject. Parents leaned on stories about birds, bees, and storks to avoid discussing the subjects of sex and human sexuality with their children. Conversations about sex took place in whispered tones around the water cooler. Many churches avoided the conversation entirely, leading many congregations to question The Episcopal Church's policies surrounding the full inclusion of LGBTQ+ persons. Times have changed. Today, sexuality is all around us: at home, on television and the Internet, at school, in the workplace, and thankfully, even in our churches.

We're disturbed by the headlines. Middle-school students are under investigation for "sexting" (pg. 70). Sexually transmitted infections are especially high in Florida, Arizona, and other locations popular with retirees due to the increased sexual activity of older adults. At a young age children are identifying themselves as transgender. Young people are bullied because of their gender identity. The gap between physical puberty and social puberty is widening. Adults are marrying later, if at all. Our vocabulary for human sexuality is rapidly expanding. These trends, and others, can lead to damaging behaviors. Because children and youth are changing the way they discuss and identify their own sexuality, the landscape of our ministry with children and youth must change as well.

Sexuality plays an important role in our lives and our society. As Christians, we recognize it as a gift from God—a gift that requires care and stewardship. It requires partnership, conversation, and support in our congregations—between children, youth, and adults of all ages. *These Are Our Bodies: Talking Faith & Sex at Church & Home* is a response to how we, as faithful communities and individuals, can address the connection between faith and our sexuality in a holistic and holy way.

ABOUT THIS BOOK

These Are Our Bodies is a theological and practical guide to conversation, grounded in the Episcopal tradition, about the complexities of sexuality in today's world. The book covers the role of sexuality in our lives in all its dimensions as well as information to guide church educators, clergy, parents, youth leaders, or anyone who seeks to broaden their knowledge on this subject. Divided into five parts, it explores the complexity of sexuality from the different perspectives of human experience: theological, ethical, biological, and practical. An extensive annotated resource section and glossary round out the book to give readers the information they need for further exploration on topics of sexuality.

Part I: The Theological includes chapters that explore the dynamic of sexuality and its connection to our faith. Richard Rohr reminds us, "the Christian religion was the only one that believed God became a human body, and yet we have had such deficient and frankly negative attitudes toward embodiment."[1] Humans are embodied people seeking to live lives that are worthy of our deep calling. How, then, do we understand the mystery of sexuality in the content of a biblical framework? Through the lens of the Baptismal Covenant, we will look at the creative nature of sexuality, the goodness of desire, and the concept of honoring the body. This section concludes with a discussion of the role of the church in the area of sexuality.

Part II: The Ethical gives us a new vocabulary necessary to expand our view of sexuality. The binary concepts of sexuality as male or female, married or single, heterosexual or homosexual are expanding. Readers will come to understand sexuality in a new way, learning new language that seeks to honor and respect the dignity of all people. Our hope is to provide the catalyst for conversations that will challenge and expand thinking about the ethical demands that call us to love our neighbor as ourselves. In light of the evolving view of sexuality, we reflect on the role of responsible behavior and models of decision-making, including consent and shaming. We finish the section with chapters that focus on the changing culture of sexuality and our call to examine stereotypes and bullying, and the inherent pain they cause.

Part III: The Biological expands on the role of parenting through childhood and adolescence, providing a review of developmental theories, moral development psychology, and faith development across a person's lifespan. Research and theories from leading psychologists underpin our understanding of what children need to develop in a healthy way—both psychologically and morally. We conclude this section with a discussion of faith development and its implications in understanding the complexity of human sexuality.

Part IV: The Practical offers adults the necessary tools to understand the stages of child development that inform our ministry with children and teens. This section also gives parents the background information they need to be the primary sexuality educators for their children. The review of development (physical, emotional and social, spiritual, and moral) will benefit anyone working with, or raising, children and teens.

Part V: Resources are rich with valuable insights and materials. The annotated resource section and glossary are a collection from the authors' reading and experience, as well as from others within The Episcopal Church community. Our hope is that readers will see this section as a jumping-off place for further learning.

USING THIS BOOK

Church leaders will be able to use this book as a general resource in linking faith and sexuality. The concepts around sexuality can inform the conversation in churches on implementing ministries that are inclusive of all persons. Youth leaders and Christian educators can use the book as a way to inform their personal ministry, as well as a guide when questions or concerns arise. Parents will find useful information in The Biological and The Practical sections, specifically.

We recognize that all **families look different**; we use "parent" in the broadest sense throughout this book. Parent refers to all those primary caretakers who have children or youth in their custody—parents, single moms, single dads, grandparents, aunts, uncles, foster parents, stepparents, LGBTQ+ parents, adoptive parents, divorced or widowed parents, and anyone else who has responsibility for raising children.

At the end of each chapter are discussion questions for starting conversations. Since each chapter has the ability to stand on its own, these questions can be used as adult-education material or with parenting groups, with participants reading a chapter prior to discussion.

We have tried our best to share current information on this subject that is evolving every day. One item you will notice is the use of pronouns when discussing gender within these pages. You may find this disconcerting as you read, but we believe it will highlight one of the limitations of the English language: Gender-specific pronouns can sometimes limit our ability to clearly speak about and with each other.

The core tenants of *These Are Our Bodies* benefit all ages, as it addresses the needs of children, youth, and adults as they navigate a world that would want them to forget who they are and whose they are. In addition to the book's use as a resource for parents and leaders, it is also designed to be an integral part of *These Are Our Bodies* human sexuality program, which is described in Part V.

WHY THIS BOOK

As a people made in the image of God, our bodies and sexuality are sacred gifts that we seek to understand and use as faithful people. Our inherent value and worth comes from God's love for us, yet our modern world is filled with sexual expression that too often leads us away from life in Christ. God loves each of God's children perfectly and works to redeem what is broken. Our faith tells us that "nothing can separate us from God's love in Christ Jesus,"[2] and our trust in

God's loving redemption gives us hope in the fulfillment of God's dream for each of us. The Church, as the family of God, can support and empower each other, including those who are parents, to engage our children (and ourselves) in deep conversations about who we are as followers of Christ—in mind, spirit, and yes, physical body.

Our responsibility as Christians to seek Christ in all persons, showing dignity and mercy to all, is rooted in our Baptismal Covenant. Our churches and communities can assist us to hear and follow our call. Families and church communities are ideal places to practice intentionally living into these promises we made at baptism, and to examine our human tendencies to ignore that call. Life reaches beyond each individual as we are shaped in communities. We form our faith within our communities: home, school, work, service, social, and church. The baptismal promises recognize that we do not grow up in life, or faith, in a vacuum; instead, we grow up influenced and shaped by those around us, while influencing and shaping them.

Christian virtues, such as respect for others, mutual sharing, patient listening, and trust in God's desire to make us whole and holy are worthy to address along with our sexuality. By seeking Christ in all persons and loving our neighbor as ourselves, our relationship with God deepens. We wish to model this behavior in all aspects of our lives, including our sexuality.

Our hope is to provide church leaders and parents with proper information and current language to create a safe space for talking about human sexuality from a faith perspective and a progressive, inclusive point of view. The foundation in writing this book is rooted in the work of The Episcopal Church's Task Force on Human Sexuality and Family Life Education (1982) that prepared a program titled *Sexuality: A Divine Gift: A Sacramental Approach to Human Sexuality and Family Life.* The following is taken from its Foreword, as we believe it continues

---

In the **Baptismal Covenant** we are asked, "Will you strive for justice and peace among all people, and respect the dignity of every human being?" Our response is, "I will, with God's help." BCP, p. 305

to be relevant today and represents the intentions of *These Are Our Bodies* as well:

> Underlying the materials presented is a point of view intended to be thought provoking, not intimidating, sensitive but not bland. Our goal is to be open to, but not enslaved by an examination of the fast paced changes and bewildering alternatives of contemporary life. We intend to be disciplined by, but not blindly submissive to, the viewpoints of our Christian forebears.[3]

With that statement in mind, we reaffirm the core beliefs as stated in *Sexuality: A Divine Gift* as being the foundation for *These Are Our Bodies*:

You are holy.
Sexuality is good.
Sexuality is powerful.
You are not alone.
You must take responsibility.[4]

Just as there are seasons to our faith (such as birth, baptism, and reaffirmation), there are seasons to our sexuality (birth, awareness, growth, change, and transformation). May the following pages help you go beyond a basic sharing of information about sex to a lifelong journey of discovery. We hope it demonstrates that a faith community, working in partnership with parents and all its members, is a trustworthy place to grow, mature, and learn about the faith connection between ones developing sexuality and God.

PART I

THE THEOLOGICAL

The whole story of creation, incarnation, and our incorporation into the fellowship of Christ's body tells us that God desires us, *as if we were God*, as if we were that unconditional response to God's giving that God's self makes in the life of the Trinity. We are created so that we may be caught up in this, so that we may grow into the wholehearted love of God by learning that God loves us as God loves God.
—Rowan D. Williams[5]

CHAPTER 1

THE MYSTERY OF SEXUALITY

As children of God we are born into the world beloved by God. We are filled with hope and promise of the future. We come into the world inherently worthy of love and awe—awe at the mystery of our holiness in who and what we are.

As we develop, our experience and our sense of self are shaped and molded by those around us. This includes our sexuality. It is inherently part of who we are; living as a sexual being is unavoidable and unavoidably complex. Sexuality is good—a gift from God since the beginning.

> Then God said, "Let us make humanity in our image to resemble us so that they may take charge of the fish of the sea, the birds in the sky, the livestock, all the earth, and all the crawling things on earth. God created humanity in God's own image, in the divine image God created them, male and female God created them. God saw everything he had made: it was supremely good."[6]

We are made in the image of God, the *Imago Dei*, a reflection of the divine. As such, there is much we will never know about our complexity and the diversity that exists within all humankind. By considering our sexuality (in essence, our true selves), we can contemplate the mysteries of human existence. To better understand human sexuality, we need to remind ourselves that "theologically we are dealing with matters at the very limits of our intellectual capacities; we are involved in profound puzzles, conundrums that we cannot solve and that we should not expect to solve."[7] It is within this context that we begin to explore human sexuality.

The overarching ethics of love, grace, and compassion serve as the foundation of our lives as faithful people, seen in the biblical theme of covenant. As a faith community, we re-tell the story of God's grace in our lives and how that unearned love compels us to love others. In Genesis, we learn that God formed a covenant with Noah and set the rainbow in the sky as a reminder of that promise. Later, we hear the call for the people to be God's people—a deep covenantal relationship through Abraham. Moses delivers the Ten Commandments to God's people while seeking the Promised Land. "The most familiar covenantal relationship is marriage, to which the Hebrew prophets and New Testament writers turned as a way to describe God's desire and commitment to be in relationship with us (Isaiah 62:5, Ephesians 5:21–33)."[8] The theme of covenant is laced throughout the Celebration and Blessing of a Marriage,[9] the Witnessing and Blessing of a Lifelong Covenant,[10] and the Witnessing and Blessing of a Marriage.[11]

In the New Covenant, Jesus Christ further reveals our sexuality as good, refocusing relationships to mutuality, respect, compassion, and hospitality. In the words of the Standing Commission on Liturgy and Music, "Baptism and Eucharist, as sacraments of God's covenant of creating, redeeming, and sustaining love, shapes our lives as Christians in relation to God and to God's creation; this calls us to live with love, compassion, justice, and peace toward all creatures, friend or foe, neighbor or stranger."[12]

LOVE AND RELATIONSHIP

Life is communal. We live in, are shaped by, and are created for relationship. As an inseparable part of us, our sexuality is part of relationships. Sexuality is powerful and we can deploy our bodies in the world in both healthy and unhealthy ways. We experience sexuality as light and shadow, as complementary opposites. Healthy sexuality is about loving and being loved, desiring and being desired, and mutual recognition of another. For many, this concept that we are created to desire and to be desired is novel.

Jesus frequently taught the concept of *agape*, or brotherly love. *Agape* is an unselfish love without sexual implications; it is the love of Christians for other persons that corresponds to the love of God for humankind—love that serves the other, embraces the other, and cares for the other. *Agape* is about relationship. This is the kind of love we see demonstrated by the Samaritan in the story of The Good Samaritan (Luke 10:25–37).

> A Samaritan, who was on a journey, came to where the man was. But when he saw him, he was moved with compassion. The Samaritan went to him and bandaged his wounds, tending them with oil and wine. Then he placed the wounded man on his own donkey, took him to an inn, and took care of him. The next day, he took two full days' worth of wages and gave them to the innkeeper. He said, "Take care of him, and when I return, I will pay you back for any additional costs." What do you think? Which one of these three was a neighbor to the man who encountered thieves?[13]

Unlike the priest and the Levite, the Samaritan went to the man who encountered the thieves. The Samaritan cared for the man's wounded body and gave unselfishly to show love and compassion, *agape*, for another person, someone he did not know. "Love of God and love of neighbor are inseparable and come alive in our lives of faith when we are able to explore and explain those commands in community."[14]

As people are created to be in relationship, scripture witnesses to this. The Gospels are filled with story after story about relationships— good and bad. Faith is about our relationship with God. Christianity is about our life and faith in relationship with God made flesh in the form of Jesus Christ. Jesus, fully divine and fully human, means that Jesus experienced life as we do—as a human with a full range of emotions, desires, and influences.

> "... **Loving our neighbors** means recognizing the body by the side of the road as a dignified human being, in need of mercy. . . . The fellow on the road to Jericho was also treated in an appalling way— as an exploitable substance, rather than a dignified human being. . . ." Katharine Jefferts Schori[15]

What we see in the whole of the scripture across time is the shift from a focus on procreation and survival to that of hospitality and mutuality. Our sexuality moves away from idolatry[16] to embracing one another in mutual recognition. God calls us into relationship with God. Adam and Eve turned away from God as they hid in the garden, yet God called out to them. The prophets, the truth-tellers, called people back to God. Even the prophets struggled with turning away and toward God. Jonah was reluctant and tried to flee from God. Jesus calls us back to God, to live in the Kingdom of God now. Jesus calls us to live in unity not through procreation, but through care and hospitality.

THE MYSTERY OF BEING HUMAN

Part of the mystery of sexuality is the mystery of humanity. Humans are capable of great and wondrous feats of valor, kindness, compassion, and caretaking as well as acts of violence and atrocities against each other. As followers of Jesus Christ we are called to love the Lord our

God with all our heart, with all our being, with all our strength, with all our mind, and love our neighbor as ourselves.[17]

"Although we sometimes identify sexuality with sexual activity and thus see sexuality as occupying a small isolated portion of our total living and being, we are foolish to deny our functioning as sexual beings. Through an understanding of the full range of love as described by C. S. Lewis (*agape, eros, storge, philia*—divine love, passion, affection, and friendship, respectively), we understand the healthy place of sexual activity and the source of sexual energy, which permeates our entire life."[18] *Agape*, that unconditional love of the other is tied to *eros*, physical love and sexual desire. To have a truly equal, vulnerable, and mutual sexual/romantic relationship one needs both. *Agape* is required for accepting people for who they are, warts and all, in all aspects. To fully recognize another person is to recognize and honor their sexuality.

At the heart of the Christian life is holiness, a call to seek and serve Christ in all persons. How can we embody the love of God, to live a life filled with faith, hope, and love? As Christians, how are we called to respond to the needs of others? Christianity is not about being right; it is about being in relationship together in Christ, striving to fulfill the gospel mandate to be one body in Christ. Faith is about a way of life. We do not all have to agree to be in relationship with each other; there is plenty of room at the table for *everyone*.

When the Church is divided "it weakens faith and witness to the gospel. Faith is weakened as attention is turned to who is right and away from the practice of faith in the love of God and neighbor."[19] In the words of the General Thanksgiving, we pray ". . . and that we show forth thy praise, not only with our lips, but in our lives, by giving up our selves to thy service, and by walking before thee in holiness and righteousness all our days."[20] Holiness is "living in and deepening the experience of God's presence in our lives together."[21]

As a people yearning to live a holy and righteous life, we are called to embrace all people with love, grace, and acceptance. All people are the children of God.

As will be discussed in Chapter 6, A New Way of Understanding Our Sexuality, sexuality is incredibly complex. Our sense of self is connected to how we feel about our bodies: physically, spiritually, emotionally, and psychologically. Our sexuality forms biologically and culturally. Much of life is complicated, multilayered, and not easily understood. Thus we need to pay particular attention to how we speak and think in terms of human sexuality. In many ways, it is a mystery that is ever unfolding before us.

Discussion Questions:

1. What does having a covenant mean to you? When have you made a promise to another person? What made it difficult (or easy) to keep?
2. What have been your most treasured relationships? What has made them special to you?
3. How can sexuality become idolatrous? Which term most describes the purpose of sexuality to you and why: procreation, survival, hospitality, mutuality, or relationship?
4. How do you care for and honor others, including their bodies?
5. Timothy Sedgwick states, holiness is "living in and deepening the experience of God's presence in our lives together." What does this mean to you?

CHAPTER 2

SEXUALITY AND OUR BAPTISMAL COVENANT

The Baptismal Covenant provides a foundation for educating all those who are a part of the Episcopal community as we strive to live as disciples of Christ through our baptismal promises and affirmations. We promise to guide and teach the newly baptized. We do not know all we need to know when we are baptized; we must continue to reexamine these promises in all aspects of our lives. Paul reminds us, "Do not be conformed to the patterns of this world, but be transformed by the renewing of your minds so that you can figure out what God's will is—what is good and pleasing and perfect."[22]

Created in the image of God by God, as Christians we are called to follow Jesus Christ, the Word made flesh.[23] God came in the form of a human to live on earth as a human. We read, hear, discuss, and use scripture as a guide to our life. Scripture is filled with sexual metaphors, sexual misconduct, sexual desire, sexuality issues such as gender inequality, and what it might mean to intentionally live life as a single person. Following Jesus's example requires a full recognition of our embodiment, a people with bodies. Jesus's healing and teaching on justice and reconciliation necessarily connects with bodies, for it is an embodied people who are redeemed and saved. If we take our baptismal promises seriously, then we must take seriously the whole of each person, recognizing their sexuality as part of one's whole personhood.

In The Episcopal Church, one or more baptized persons sponsor each candidate, who may be a child or an adult, for Holy Baptism. At every baptism, in addition to sponsors, godparents, and parents, the community makes promises to the newly baptized that have implications for how we live our lives in the world. Anne Kitch writes:

> With each new baptism, not only does the newly baptized embark on this life of faith, but the members of the Christian community recommit themselves to this journey as well. They promise once again to grow in their understanding of God's will for them, to develop a moral stance based on the teachings of Christ, and to become more loving people. Life for the baptized is not lived in isolation but is intentionally placed in the context of the Christian community.[24]

Community is central to baptism and to a life of faith. Our baptismal promises indicate that we are not alone in this world. Instead, we are ever loved; our community supports us. Kitch says, "the congregation is there to help the parents and godparents remember what they said they would do. The congregation promises to support the parents and godparents as well as the children about to be baptized."[25] Every time a child is baptized, not only do we welcome that child into the fold, but we also promise to support and help parents as they raise their child. We make these promises as individuals but also as a community. And these promises are lifelong.

"The Baptismal Covenant commits Christians to living out their baptism in their daily lives."[26] The church must be open to God's presence, open to God's help. Perhaps one of the ways we receive God's help is through the support of others during a critical time in our life. "As a community of faith and nurture, the church is called upon to teach and transmit those sexual meanings it finds consonant with Christian faith."[27] If honoring the body is a shared practice *and* the church is called to teach and transmit sexual meanings congruent with Christian faith, then the church must provide opportunities for conversation with each other. The church must also provide scientifically, medically accurate, up-to-date information. Every body is worthy of love, care, respect, and blessing.

STRIVING FOR JUSTICE

Much of our conversation in the Church has been reactive rather than affirmative. Issues of sexuality have been brought to the forefront the past two decades due to sexual misconduct scandals in the Roman Catholic Church. As a result, denominations have greatly improved their protective measures for ministry with vulnerable populations through better awareness training for volunteers.

Every denomination has struggled with how to move forward with ordination rights and marriage rights for LGBTQ+ individuals and couples. The Episcopal Church has suffered splits in congregations and in dioceses over these issues and understandings of human sexuality. For many the discernment and conversations continue. However, the resolution on same-sex blessings[28] and the approval of liturgies for same-sex blessings and marriages became a reality at the General Convention in 2015.[29]

Much of these conversations have been rooted in studying the theological implications of the Baptismal Covenant. The covenant asks, "Will you seek and serve Christ in all persons, loving your neighbor as yourself?" and "Will you strive for justice and peace and respect the dignity of every human being?" Cameron Partridge, Episcopal chaplain at Harvard writes:

> These may well be the words most often cited in Episcopal Church conversation about LGBTQI people. The call to respect the human dignity of LGBTQI people and to strive for justice on their behalf is considered by many Episcopalians to be fundamental to their baptismal identities.[30]

The acronym **LGBTQ+** stands for Lesbian, Gay, Bi-Sexual, Transgender, Queer, Questioning, Intersex, and Asexual. Some like to also include Ally.

The United States has experienced bitter battles over equal marriage rights for partnered gay and lesbian citizens with many of the arguments based on people's interpretation of scripture. The debate about the rights of gays and lesbians across denominations demonstrates that the Church is not of one voice on sexuality. Nevertheless, the debate also demonstrates how much the Church needs to discuss sexuality.

Our understandings of sexuality in the culture and in the Church have changed over the centuries. For example, the term "sodomy" does not appear in scripture, but coalesced exclusively around a particular sexual act between men only in the eleventh century.[31] Homosexuality, from the Greek meaning "same," was once a term used to classify certain people. We now understand one's sexual orientation can be on a continuum: straight, lesbian, gay, bisexual, and transgender. All of this continues to vex politicians and religious leaders alike. How to think theologically and spiritually about the diversity of human sexuality and gender remains a vital concern for Christian churches today, but only for discerning the moral status of differently gendered sexual practices. Addressing this topic evokes a much wider constellation of concerns for Christian faith communities.[32]

Former Archbishop of Canterbury Rowan Williams stresses that sexuality related issues are bound up with our politics, social recreation, and justice.[33] The fact that people spend millions of dollars on political campaigns arguing theological understandings of same-sex marriage demonstrates that our sexuality is inextricably tied to our politics and our sense of justice. Sexuality education in the church provides a space for people to discuss the implications of our understanding of sexuality such as sexuality of singles, older adults, and LGBTQ+ issues in a meaningful way, as well as with children and youth.

The voice of the gospel and the life of Jesus is an ever-changing inspiration as people hear the call of the good news in their own lives. The Bible is central to the understanding of moral and just living. Exegesis and interpretation are necessary to take the Bible very seriously, yet not literally. In the area of sexual ethic, the Hebrew Bible provides the guiding image of humans being made in the image of God. The New Testament gives an overt command to love God and neighbor. The command to love God and neighbor is also seen in our call to work for justice for all. Although scripture provides a call to us in our Christian walk, the guide is not prescriptive.

As the Body of Christ, we have come to interpret Holy Scripture in the life and witness of our lives and the call to spread the good news of the Gospel. Reinterpreting scripture is an ancient practice. The Jewish rabbis loosened and bound the law—expanding and constricting the law as situations changed. Jesus, the rabbi, did the same. Jesus reinterpreted the law when he walked through the fields to defend gleaning on the Sabbath. Jesus stood for all people above the adherence to the law. In the twentieth century, The Episcopal Church also continued the tradition of hearing the Bible as it is speaking to a new generation. When the call of women to the ordained priesthood was considered, the Church went back into the Hebrew Scriptures and the New Testament and found examples of female leaders. Looking at tradition, scripture, and reason, The Episcopal Church (as well as other denominations) was called to change, to move to inclusion.

Today the inclusion of LGBTQ+ persons has once again led us to examine our interpretation of scripture and to look to the example of Jesus's life and teaching. As The Episcopal Church moves farther along the path of full inclusion for all, there are many, including fellow Anglicans who continue to assert that The Episcopal Church has made a radical departure from the teaching of Scripture. For many people these declarations cause great pain. The LGBTQ+ community has been a tireless witness to the love of Christ in this world and has worked through prayer and advocacy to have their voice heard as equal. William Countryman says it well, when he speaks of the division in the Anglican Communion:

> In the same way, no voice in contemporary Anglicanism can reconcile those who feel that the existence of gay, lesbian, and transgender Anglicans is radically transgressive with those who are persuaded that it is an important victory of the gospel.[34]

A victory of the gospel! What an affirmation of faith and of justice. As the gospel message of freedom, inclusion, and love continues to work in this world and in the hearts of people, we recognize the LGBTQ+ community as having full equality. Of course, in God's eye, they have always been loved and accepted—it is we humans who needed to catch onto the press of God's justice in the world. The gospel and the life of Jesus will continue to disturb our lives and our hearts for justice. As our hearts transform, so will the world.

Conversation and education about sex, sexuality, and sexual ethics are issues of justice. The way we talk about sex and our embodied spirits and inspirited bodies matters. How we talk about these issues, or remain silent, can lead to justice or injustice.

Without discussion about sexuality, about living as embodied people, the Church will continue to struggle in the most divisive ways. Joyce Ann Mercer tells us that girls continue to wrestle with internalized gender oppression. The "Boy Code," which teaches boys they must repress and not share or express feelings that may be deemed "feminine," is alive and well.[35] Girls receive a message that they must have large breasts, but be thin. Adolescents are grappling with body image and the spiritual harm done when they try to divorce body and soul.[36]

By participating in and facilitating discussions about sexuality and how to live into our embodied selves, the Church has the opportunity to shift to a culture of civil discourse—creating a culture where all people can come to the table for discussion, to be fed literally and spiritually. The Church can be the place where all people can be honored and loved simply because they were created in the image of God, loved by God, desired by God.[37]

Discussion Questions:

1. How was sexuality discussed in your family when you were growing up? What, if anything, do you wish had been different?
2. What is the obligation of a faith community for sharing and interpreting issues of sexuality together, across generations?
3. How have you been able to reflect, theologically and spiritually, about the diversity of human sexuality and gender in our society today? Where have you struggled? What questions remain for you?

CHAPTER 3

THE BODY AS SACRED

As a place for moral and ethical discussions with theological underpinnings, the Church is positioned to have broad discussions about the sacred meaning of the body. If the Church takes seriously the vows of the Baptismal Covenant, then "we must be the supportive community in which the newly baptized will develop as members of the Body of Christ."[38]

Scripture looks beyond our sexuality as merely reproductive and places humanity as the object of God's desiring. Sexual metaphors throughout scripture describe God's relationship to humanity, providing a broader sense of meaning behind desiring. We are relational *and* bodied beings. Our bodies are sexual, and our bodies connect us to each other in collaboration, community, language, culture, and politics.

Our bodies matter to God. Stephanie Paulsell articulates this in her explanation of the incarnation:

The affirmation that every body is made in the image of God is supplemented in Christianity by the belief that God was somehow fully present in a particular human body that lived in a particular time and place, the body of Jesus of Nazareth. The church has used the word *incarnation* to describe the conviction that God was *incarnate*, enfleshed in a body that ate and drank, slept and woke, touched and received touch. This body also suffered a death as painful and degrading as any human beings have devised. Early Christian testimony that this body also lived again after death shapes a profound Christian hope that undergirds the practice of honoring the body. Whatever else it means, the Resurrection of Jesus suggests that bodies matter to God. And they ought to matter to us.[39]

BODY *AND* SOUL

Hebrew and Christian views of body and soul have been in conflict for quite a long time. In the Hebrew Scriptures, the whole person is *both* body and soul—the undivided self. In the ancient Christian view, as well as current interpretations, the soul is the highest, finest aspect of being human and the body is regarded as a prison cell trapping the soul.[40] This idea of a divided self gave rise and opportunity to suppress bodily function and desires. Richard Rohr reflects on his deep disappointment:

> . . . [T]hat the Christian religion was the only one that believed God became a human body, and yet we have had such deficient and frankly negative attitudes toward embodiment, the physical world, sexuality, emotions, animals, wonderful physical practices like yoga, and nature itself. We want to do spirituality all in the head. It often seems to me that Western Christianity has been much more formed by Plato (body and soul are at war) than by Jesus (body and soul are already one). For many of us, the body is more *repressed and denied*

than even the mind or the heart. It makes both presence and healing quite difficult, because the body, not just our mind, holds our memories.[41]

The Church is being called to reclaim the connectedness and wholeness of body, mind, and soul. By learning how the Christian tradition gives shape to the practice of honoring the body and learning to honor the sacredness of our own bodies, we can better honor the sacredness of others and others' bodies.

Sexuality is part of humanness, part of our spiritual selves, and the body is more than sex, more than sexuality. "Embodiment is a sacred gift."[42] Karen Lebacqz writes about how the "thou shalt not" Christian culture strongly conflicts with the "thou shalt" contemporary culture where sex is encouraged and there is tremendous pressure to engage in sexual activity.[43] "The sexual body does not exist apart from the body that eats and drinks, bathes and dresses, rests and exercises and works. Sexual desire does not exist in isolation from other desires. It is only through learning to honor the body in every aspect of our embodied life that we will be able to honor our bodies' sexual feelings and desires."[44] As people of faith, we see sex and sexuality as natural parts of humanness; the desire and need for physical touch draws us to other people.

In the twenty-first century, we are living in a culture of casual sex that teaches us to separate the physical body from emotion, creating a false sense that we are not, nor do we need to be, vulnerable when engaging in sexual activity. "Sex between people who do not love one another and are not willing to become uniquely responsible to and for one another assumes a split between body and spirit that does not exist. When we have sex, all of who we are is on the line. Any attempt to deploy our bodies in a sexual encounter while holding back the rest of our selves damages us; the impossible attempt to divide body and spirit does violence to both."[45]

In the United States, popular media presents a false narrative of self-fulfillment and pleasure as the ultimate goal. Therefore, in a world increasingly focused on separating our physical selves from our psychological and spiritual selves, the Church must claim sexuality in positive terms. The Church's narrative of freedom in Christ reminds us that we are honored and valued, body and soul.

Treating the body as sacred is about our whole being. "God created our bodies good. God dwelled fully in a vulnerable human body. In death God gathers us up—body and all. Through our bodies we participate in God's activity in the world."[46] By examining the importance of honoring the body and the ways we are to treat each other, the Church can better help individuals make healthy decisions about relationships and how we deploy our bodies into the world.

HONORING THE BODY IN COMMUNITY

Honoring the body is a shared practice. People need guidance and support from their family, friends, and communities that openly affirm and articulate sexuality as good. Many parents of the current generation and generations before did not grow up in families or communities that openly discussed or affirmed sexuality, which may contribute to their anxiety in talking with their children about their bodies. Thus they are looking for new ways to engage their families in meaningful conversations around sexuality. Adults, especially parents, benefit from participating in sexuality education programs by receiving positive body information they did not receive growing up. Additionally, congregations offering sexuality education provide a support group of sorts for parents as they have an opportunity to discuss difficult issues with other parents.

These shared experiences shape parents, how they think about sexuality, and how they discuss sexuality with their children. James Nelson describes humans as "human *becomings*" because we create symbols, attach meaning to these symbols, and interpret them. Our meanings are socially constructed, changed, and modified through social interaction. God created us in and for community. "Communities exist by shared symbols, language, communication, and meanings. And that is the essence of our sexuality."[47] By sharing and interpreting issues of sexuality together, parents are shaping the community that is shaping them and their child. (See the discussion of the cultural and social aspects of human development on pages 103–4.)

Discussion Questions:

1. How do you feel desired by God?
2. Richard Rohr speaks of a "divided self" having roots in Christianity. In what ways have you separated your emotions, sexuality, intellect, and physical being?
3. How do you honor your body?

CHAPTER 4

CONVERSATIONS GROUNDED IN A FAITH COMMUNITY

Education and growth are lifelong endeavors. The Church provides a unique opportunity for all ages of people to come together to discuss important societal and spiritual issues.

Making the connection between our Christian call and our bodies enables intentional and faithful living. Offering the same health and medically accurate information that schools may provide to our children (acknowledging that not all school systems offer such education), we can reinforce their secular education in the context of our faith. We recognize that parents are the primary sexuality educators for their children. We can discuss gender roles, sexual messages in the media, and values that are widespread. We are also in a position to help parents start these conversations at a very young age, truly making conversations about sexuality, caring for our bodies, and caring for the bodies of others a lifelong conversation.

The earlier a parent starts these conversations and includes value statements, the easier it will be for the upcoming generation to have these important conversations with each other and their children. In addition to differences in each of our sexuality, churches are also in a position to help, not only parents, but also everyone, by modeling how we care for those who are differently abled, the ill, and the aging.

PARTNERING WITH PARENTS

The Church has the opportunity to empower and support parents through the anxiety-ridden experience of openly discussing sexuality with tweens. We have the environment to bring parents together to share stories and be in community together, to know they are not alone. We are free to discuss "big questions" and support teenagers' heightened search for meaning and God. We can provide a place for families to have conversation about their values, which inform how people perceive their sexuality. We are able to guide children and youth through the gender challenges facing them such as girls' internalized gender oppression. We can examine the stories of our faith in connection to our culture that form and shape how women view themselves in the world. We can help break the "boy code"[48] by providing a space where boys are free, in fact encouraged, to express their emotions, to be vulnerable, to find solitude, and to connect their body and soul.

We can model safe, healthy, appropriate relationships by providing adult conversation partners. We can freely and openly talk about desire in all of its forms. We can empower parents to be the primary sexuality educators of their children. We can continue to care for older adults' aging bodies. We can model a positive sexuality, a positive embodied being for all ages. We can continue to demonstrate that God desires us, God loves us, and God created us as whole people, body and soul together.

Our churches are a natural place where boys and girls have access to people of all ages, access to married and single adults, and exposure to many examples of gender identity. There are opportunities to practice a variety of skills and observe skill levels with chances to lead and to watch various types of leaders. Both boys and girls can explore gender identity and connect their sexuality with their faith. Within the context of a diverse community, we can focus on building and sustaining long-term relationships across generations.

If congregations have not provided opportunities for sexuality education, the most effective place to start is counterintuitive—beginning with young families at the commencement of their journey; families lay a foundation for the later, more complex adolescent years. However, in reality, any place we start the conversation is a great place to start. Hopefully every age group has an opportunity to explore the spiritual, cultural, social, and relational aspects of sexuality. Young adults, divorced adults, single adults, older adults, committed couples all may have very different views on how they experience norms around issues of sexuality, especially from those norms of adolescents and their parents. Every age and stage is important and should have space in the congregation for conversation, including children.

ADOLESCENTS NEED ADULTS

Many people believe that young people are not interested in God or religion. It is true that mainline churches in the United States are shrinking in size, including Episcopal congregations. The "nones" have conflicting views about organized religion's impact on society. They view religious institutions as performing good works, but they [churches] are too concerned with money and power, too involved in politics, and too focused on rules.[49] Many people, young and old, claim to be spiritual rather than religious because of the stereotypes laid upon them when people identify themselves as part of a religious community.

Nevertheless, faith is still important to roughly half of U.S. teenagers.[50] Additionally, churches are still the largest provider of programs to teenagers. In addition to offering programming for adults to learn about and discuss their theological questions, the Church needs to incorporate children, teens, and young adults into the life of the parish to connect them with adults who love them, care for them, and can help them address their deep theological questions.

In her qualitative research study, Dr. Mercer interviewed fifty **adolescent girls** who share "how they think about, experience, and express spiritual and religious meanings in their lives." She focuses her analysis on four areas in relation to the girls' spiritual life: faith, gender, the girl's relationship to her mother, and her relationship to her father. Mercer's key findings are: Girls want adult conversation partners on the topic of their faith life; girls need help discerning gender justice issues; parents play a huge role in their daughters' spiritual lives; girls actively make meaning in relation to faith and want their faith to make a difference in the world.

Invitations to discuss sexuality with other adults provide adolescents with additional adults and role models in their lives.

In *Girl Talk, God Talk*, Joyce Ann Mercer shares how girls express their desire for adult conversation partners. "In many different ways, however, they also said that they long for adult faith mentors. They wanted mothers, fathers, and other adults in their lives to think critically with them about faith questions. They wanted to push—and have someone respectfully push back. They wanted to be able to ask 'big questions' and search for meaning in the company of adults as well as in the company of their peers."[51] Our challenge, as a society and church, is to connect young people in particular to morally admirable adults:

What really holds potential for making a moral impact on a mid-adolescent is a powerful connection with individual adults whom he can admire or idealize. It is that individual teacher, coach, counselor, religious youth worker, Big Brother, neighbor, stepparent, grandparent, police officer, or other individuals in the community who can inspire him to make moral sense of the social confusion or his surrounding.[52]

The Church has the unique opportunity to connect young people to a variety of adults of various ages to explore their moral questions.

Adolescents are embarking on the incredibly difficult journey of learning to develop friendships, romantic relationships, puberty, finding their voice, identity, body image, soul, and developing decision-making skills. All these topics fit well into the overarching call of equipping and empowering disciples in the world.

BUILDING A CONTAINER FOR LIFE

The stories of our faith bind us together over time and space. Anne Kitch reminds us that our baptism binds us together as the Body of Christ, called to grow in [our] understanding of God's will for [us], to develop a moral stance based on the teachings of Christ, and to become a more loving people.[53] There is space at the table and space in the river Jordan for all to participate in the conversation, even if we do not agree. We are not called to be of one mind; we are called, with God's help, to love our neighbors and to respect the dignity of every human being.

Honoring the body recognizes and embraces humans as sexual beings. Our bodies physically carry us through life, helping us engage and make sense of the world. We cannot separate one part of our bodies from another; therefore, we cannot separate our sexuality from our bodies. Our body, our sexuality, our whole person is worthy of honor. Stephanie Paulsell writes:

> Young people who have grown up learning that the body mirrors back to us something important about God and that the body's desires are a precious gift from God worthy of being sheltered and allowed to develop in freedom have a compass to help them negotiate the road to sexual maturity. Adolescence will never be easy. And our world holds dangers that are sometimes beyond our power to control. But young people who have learned to honor their bodies in every other aspect of their lives will be more convinced that their bodies and the bodies of others are deserving of honor in their sexual lives as well. They will be better equipped to resist that which would diminish them or constrain their freedom to become the people they were meant to be, and better able to embrace that which would enlarge their

spirits and nurture an ever more loving engagement with the world.[54]

In *Falling Upward* Richard Rohr writes about the two halves of life. The task of the first half is for us to build a "container" to hold the contents of the second half of life. We build this "container" by struggling with law, tradition, custom, authority, boundaries, and morality, as we have to have something hard and half-good to rebel against. The first half of life is hard enough. We have an opportunity to help those in the first half of life build a strong enough "container." We have an essential voice and obligation to provide sexuality education to all people. With intentionality, openness, faithfulness, and most importantly with God's help, we can build a better, healthier embodied present and future.

Discussion Questions:

1. How would you like your faith community to support you in having conversations with your children, teens, or partners about sexuality?
2. What adult mentors did you have as a child or teen? What insights or learnings did you glean from those relationships?
3. What "container" do you wish to build for your child?

CHAPTER 5

SEXUALITY EDUCATION HONORS THE BODY

Our bodies are an indispensible part of who we are. We cannot take off or put on our bodies.[55] Parents, teachers, mentors, and role models freely and willingly talk about how we are in the world and how we care about ourselves. We strive to teach future generations basic life and safety skills such as wearing a seatbelt at all times in a vehicle, the dangers of tobacco and illicit drug use, the importance of good nutrition and moving our body daily. Our bodies need much to be sustained in this world. We require fruits and vegetables, water, movement, sleep, and touch among other things. Sexuality education, whether we know it or like it, is included in this list. Sexuality education aids people in learning and using skills that enable them to embrace and affirm the wholeness of their sexuality and to talk openly and honestly about a connection between their sexuality and faith.

The community and the Body of Christ benefit from people who practice an understanding of sexuality that is positive and accepting. As we learn by reflecting on our lives—the successes and failures—while trusting in God's blessings and forgiveness, we acknowledge the Spirit's desire to "guide (us) in all truth."[56]

THE ROLE OF CULTURE

In recent years our culture has seen an outpouring of articles, news stories, and emergence of sex educators and sex writers. We are surrounded by sex in our culture and have access to an overwhelming amount of information. We hear an outcry from various communities regarding sexual behavior affecting people's lives in challenging ways. For example, from the higher education community, sexual assaults are bringing greater exposure to issues surrounding alcohol consumption, rape culture, and consent. Young people are challenging the use of limited language around gender identity and sexual orientation.

Study after study has shown the most effective sexual education is science-based, and yet an overwhelming number of young adults and older generations feel uncomfortable and embarrassed to talk about sex and sexuality. Fear of teaching people correct, medically accurate terminology and information only perpetuates the problems many have with body shame and ignorance. Medically accurate terminology and information helps people to understand all the parts of their body, how they work, and how to stay healthy without the sting of shame or fear.

Young adults and adolescents are pushing society to engage in a different conversation about sex and sexuality than the conversations offered in the past. They are asking for better ways to discuss our bodies, what it means to be a sexual person, and sex. For example, Laci Green is a twenty-something sex educator activist who began her work as a sex educator on YouTube while still in college as a response "to what [she believes] to be a nationwide failure to provide comprehensive sex education and to adopt healthy, realistic attitudes about sexuality."[57] Al Vernacchio is a long-time high-school sexual educator in Pennsylvania who has become well known and respected around the country for his writings in the *New York Times*, his book *For Goodness Sex: Changing the Way We Talk to Teens about Sexuality, Values, and Health* (New York: Harper Wave, 2014) and his popular TED Talk from March 2012, "Sex needs a new metaphor. Here's one . . ."[58] His writing and TED Talk is straightforward, approachable, and filled with humor. In his TED Talk he shifts the metaphor of one of competition: baseball, to one that is universally understood and non-competitive: pizza.

THE ROLE OF PARENTS AND OTHER ADULTS

Parents are their children's primary sex educators. The people around us teach us about our value and our worth. How we feel about our body shapes many other aspects in our lives and vice versa. Just as we cannot separate love of God from love of neighbor, our bodies are inseparable from the rest of our lives and should be treated as such. Our bodies are an essential part of who we are and how we express ourselves. Our bodies are vulnerable and need our care and protection.

The adults who raise us are our primary educators about our (and others') sexuality. They teach us how to care for, talk about, and use our bodies. They model, consciously and unwittingly, behaviors and attitudes that will form our opinions on what is good and bad in terms of sexuality. We experience the world through our senses. But we also learn about the world through our lens of interpretation that is shaped by our previous experiences and those around us. This is a continuous process, happening throughout our lives.

Communication and openness between children and the adults raising them is critical. These adults have a great influence over their views about sexuality, puberty, body development, friendships, love relationships, and more. Talking with children about any of these topics does not have to be anxiety producing. Talking about sexuality and all that comes along with it is important; not having open conversation teaches children that sexuality and being a sexual being is something to fear, ignore, and be ashamed of. Many excellent resources exist to help parents talk with their children.

Sexuality is: ". . . a central aspect of being human throughout life encompasses sex, gender identities and roles, sexual orientation, eroticism, pleasure, intimacy and reproduction. Sexuality is experienced and expressed in thoughts, fantasies, desires, beliefs, attitudes, values, behaviors, practices, roles and relationships. While sexuality can include all of these dimensions, not all of them are always experienced or expressed. Sexuality is influenced by the interaction of biological, psychological, social, economic, political, cultural, legal, historical, religious and spiritual factors."[59]

In Part IV: The Practical, teachable moments and answers for tough questions are offered.

THE ROLE OF THE CHURCH

Sexuality education focuses on all of what makes us, us—how we feel about our body, how we interact with other people, our sexual orientation, our gender identity, and our sexual expression and attraction. Talking about our sexuality in the Church is essential as our sexuality informs our faith, and our faith informs our sexuality. If Christians believe that God came in the flesh, in fully human form, then our sexuality has everything to do with our faith, and our faith has everything to do with our sexuality.

To be human is to be a person of paradox, complication, simplicity, and feelings including . . . sadness and despair, great hope and expectation. There is an iconic picture in American Christian culture of the laughing Jesus. Christian scripture tells stories of a Jesus who demonstrates great compassion,[60] expresses great despair,[61] and shows great anger.[62] Jesus, in his humanness, is an example of embracing the fullness of our humanness. Jesus experienced the world through his body—using all of his senses to express emotion, connection, and love. Jesus's life is filled with stories that depict care for the body: stories of washing, eating, community, rest, caring for the sick and dying.

This is also seen in the doctrines of the Christian faith. "Convictions about creation, incarnation, and resurrection hold the body at the center of Christian life, where it influences how Christians worship and how Christians understand themselves."[63]

Throughout history the story of Jesus's sexuality, maleness, or possibility of marriage relationships have been sanitized. However, the whole of scripture is not sanitized. Scripture includes stories of awful atrocities against other people along with powerful stories of love and desire. To embrace and affirm the wholeness of sexuality is to embrace and affirm the wholeness of who we are. It recognizes that we are not only flesh. It recognizes that we are more than emotion. It recognizes that we are made to be in relationship with ourselves and with each other. We are made to be in relationships with God and each other; we are body, mind, and soul.

In *Honoring the Body*, Stephanie Paulsell states the importance of young adults having a variety of places to go where their desires and body are welcomed and discussed. The Church can model and support families by respecting young persons' desires as well as their bodies. Installing changing stations in all bathrooms, regardless of gender, is an example of embracing people, body and soul. Inviting discussion and support groups for older adults who are adjusting to their changing bodies provides a connection between our sexuality and faith. The Church can provide a place for honoring and caring for bodies of all ages and abilities: a place that embraces and affirms the wholeness of who we are.

BEING REALISTIC AND RELEVANT

We must examine what our tradition and theology says about sexuality. The Church must work to meet the developmental needs of each age group by understanding the societal pressures upon them in addition to their physical, cognitive, and spiritual development. We must be realistic and directly address difficult topics of sexuality instead of continuing to stay silent. For example, we have learned there are significant biological, physiological, and cognitive differences between males and females; we must not only recognize these differences, but also honor them in how we teach and the opportunities we provide.

We are called to listen to the language we (and others) use as it is shaped by our ever-changing culture. For example, a trainer recently spoke about using the terms boy-ness and girl-ness in a workshop she recently led. Some of the participants were offended by the use of "old" terminology. While the terminology used was only a couple of years old, the language had already shifted.

The Church is poised for meaningful discussion about the sacred meaning of the body. One way to live out our baptismal promises to love and serve our community is to provide young and old with the information they need to help them honor their body and their sexuality.

Discussion Questions:

1. What do you believe are the most important components of a sexuality education program?
2. Where, when, and with whom did you receive your sexuality education?
3. Who do you think should be providing sexual education to today's children and youth?
4. What is your definition of "sexuality"?
5. Do you believe your body is sacred? Why or why not?

PART II

THE
ETHICAL

Human sexuality, however, is more than a cosmic, vital force. Sexuality is also a language of mutual recognition. What is desired is not simply the body but the life formed together, a desire for love.[64]

—Timothy Sedgwick

CHAPTER 6

A NEW WAY OF UNDERSTANDING OUR SEXUALITY

As Episcopalians we recognize both the physical experience and the inward grace in both the sacraments of the Church and in our daily lives. Scripture provides an understanding that "our sexuality is a *gift* from God, a gift that calls us to relationship and concern for each other. From the creation account in Genesis to the unabashed sensuality of the Song of Songs (The Song of Solomon) and the assertion of Paul that wives and husbands may claim each other's bodies as their own, our biblical tradition affirms our sexual nature."[65]

In God we see both feminine and masculine characteristics. Therefore, we must acknowledge the androgyny of God. "We need not be trapped into speculating about the 'gender' or the 'sexuality' of God; we do need to acknowledge that none of the images is completely satisfactory or sufficient, so that male and female and nonsexual images are all required, if we are to say what we want to say about God."[66] As people seeking to live a life filled with grace for others, and ourselves, we must begin to change our nomenclature around gender and sexuality.

THE LANGUAGE WE USE

In the United States we talk about sexuality as binary—two opposing parts—our sex as either male or female and our gender as either man or woman. The following models help provide a visual of the complicated overlay of several spectrums that create the complete sense of our sexuality. People are not binary sexual beings as we are all born man and woman; even our sex assigned at birth is not strictly binary as some people are born intersex. Over time through preference, experience, and culture we figure out where we situate ourselves on each spectrum.

The Genderbread Person[67] gives us a new model for understanding the continuum of sexuality. In the past we have named homosexuality and heterosexuality as normative. Yet, we know that sexuality is more complicated than a single continuum. The Genderbread Person helps us to see the complexity of sexuality through the perspective of biological sex, gender, sexual orientation, and expression. There are multiple planes to understanding the diversity within God's beautifully created world. The understanding of our sexuality is a personal one; each of these expressions is claimed and identified for ourselves, not named and imposed by others.

The **gender binary** is the classification of sex and gender into two distinct, opposite and disconnected forms of masculine and feminine. It is one general type of gender system. Binary is used as an adjective to describe the genders female/male or woman/man. Since the binary genders are the only ones recognized by general society as being legitimate, they enjoy an unfairly privileged status.

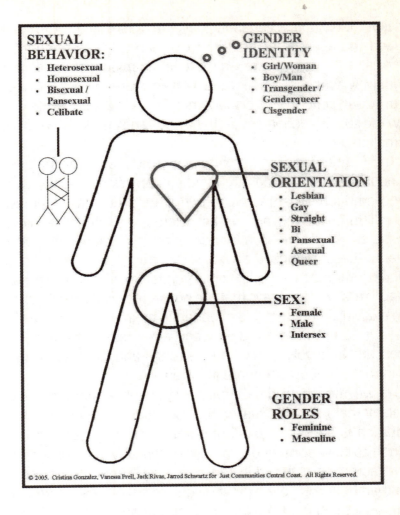

SEXUAL BEHAVIOR:
- Heterosexual
- Homosexual
- Bisexual / Pansexual
- Celibate

GENDER IDENTITY
- Girl/Woman
- Boy/Man
- Transgender / Genderqueer
- Cisgender

SEXUAL ORIENTATION
- Lesbian
- Gay
- Straight
- Bi
- Pansexual
- Asexual
- Queer

SEX:
- Female
- Male
- Intersex

GENDER ROLES
- Feminine
- Masculine

Our biological sex is the anatomical and physiological understanding of ourselves and includes our genetic characteristics of being male or female. Do our bodies have male or female genitalia? And how does each person identify themselves on a scale between male and female? Gender is both our gender identity and our gender expression. Gender identity is our psychological sense of being, such as male, female, and genderqueer. Gender expression is the way a person interprets their gender with outward displays of that gender based on the cultural norms that define feminine and masculine behavior. "Individuals generally develop a sense of their gender between the ages of 18 months to 3 years."[68] Do we identify as a male or as a female? Or are we more in the middle of the continuum and identify with both male and female stereotypes? How do we interpret our gender and display that to the outside world? Do we follow the socially defined roles, behaviors, and appearances assigned to females and males?

The Gender Unicorn[69] provides another model for the sexuality continuum. For gender identity, gender expression, sexually attracted to, and emotionally attracted to, we situate ourselves somewhere along all three of the arrows associated with each category. For example, many people have friends who are women, men, and other genders. These friends are people to whom we are emotionally attracted. Another example using gender expression: People may engage in the world in ways that are not stereotypical for their gender. As an example, one person's experience might be as follows: "When I was a little girl I preferred to wear lacy dresses, have ribbons in my hair, and be involved in whatever rough-and-tumble activities the boys in the neighborhood were involved in."

As we moved from a binary way of understanding sexuality (female or male, homosexual or heterosexual), a closer look at sexual orientation is needed. Sexual orientation, in a limited definition, is confined to how someone expresses themselves or to whom they are attracted. In a broader sense, sexual orientation is so much more than how you act or to who you are sexually attracted. Sexual orientation is distinct from the other components of sex and gender, including biological sex, gender identity, and gender expression. The American Psychological Association discusses sexual orientation in their *Answers to Your Questions: For a Better Understanding of Sexual Orientation & Homosexuality*:

Sexual orientation is commonly discussed as if it were solely a characteristic of an individual. This perspective is incomplete because sexual orientation is defined in terms of relationships with others. People express their sexual orientation through

The Gender Unicorn

Graphic by: TSER — Trans Student Educational Resources

To learn more go to:
www.transstudent.org/gender

Design by Landyn Pan
Illustration by Anna Moore

behaviors with others, including such simple actions as holding hands or kissing. Thus, sexual orientation is closely tied to the intimate personal relationships that meet deeply felt needs for love, attachment, and intimacy. In addition to sexual behaviors, these bonds include nonsexual physical affection between partners, shared goals and values, mutual support, and ongoing commitment. Therefore, sexual orientation is not merely a personal characteristic within an individual. Rather, one's sexual orientation defines the group of people in which one is likely to find the satisfying and fulfilling romantic relationships that are an essential component of personal identity for many people.[70]

These terms are not all inclusive of the complex concept of sexuality. Different models offer alternative conceptualizations, constructs, or variations of this model. Human sexuality forms in different ways and can be anywhere along the continuum. Some people move along the continuum their whole lives.

Gender identity refers to our innate, deeply felt sense of being male, female, both, or neither. It can be different from the biological sex we are assigned at birth. Many people who are living this experience refer to themselves as "transgender." What most people find difficult is to differentiate between gender and gender identity.

Sexuality Continuum

Biological sex is how we are defined as female, male, or intersex. It describes our internal and external bodies—including our sexual and reproductive anatomy, our genetic makeup, and our hormones.

Gender refers to society's expectations about how we should think and act as girls and boys, and women and men. It is our biological, social, and legal status as women and men.

Gender expression is how one conveys their gender and gender roles through clothing, behavior, and personal appearance.

Gender identity is one's perception of the social category to which they belong, for example being male, female, neither, or both.

Genderqueer are those who do not feel that they fit into the traditional, Western two-gender system. Reasons for identifying as genderqueer vary.

Romantic attraction is the interest that makes people desire romantic contact or interaction with another person or persons.

It names whether we are attracted to either males or females. Again, on a continuum that includes an understanding that attraction can be fluid between exclusively male and exclusively female with an understanding of attractions to both males and females in the center of the continuum.

Romantic orientation describes an individual's pattern of romantic attraction based on a person's gender(s) regardless of one's sexual orientation. For individuals who experience sexual attraction, their sexual orientation and romantic orientation are often in alignment (i.e., they experience sexual attraction toward individuals of the same gender(s) as the individuals they are interested in forming romantic relationships with).

Sexual attraction is the pull that makes people desire sexual contact or show sexual interest in another person(s).

Transgender means a person whose gender identity is different from their biological sex.

See more at www.plannedparenthood.org

Gender (masculine and feminine) is a social construct that socially defines roles for men and women. These may differ from culture to culture. Individual gender identity, however, is set in the brain before a child is born and guides the child in how to behave and interact with others. When the physical sex and gender identity do not match, it creates confusion, tension, and anxiety within and between the individuals and their surrounding community. The means of resolving this tension varies. Some will be driven to seek relief through surgery, bringing body into harmony with the brain. Others will find that harmony through alternative means of gender expression, such as what they wear and what pronouns they use.

Not everyone succeeds, often resulting in deepening depression and suicide attempts—frequently the first sign that something is drastically wrong. How do we support and provide assistance to transgender people who often find themselves ostracized by family, even by their own religious communities? How do we welcome them into our church?

RADICAL HOSPITALITY

Living in a radical hospitality of grace and love will spread the light of Christ into our communities of faith and show people that they are welcomed and loved. We can also move beyond a passive welcome to actually preparing for people who identify as transgender in our congregations.

One of the biggest battlefields upon which the fight for transgender rights is taking place daily are in restrooms. It seems that every other week a transgender child is made the center of a national news story because they used the restroom assigned to the gender they identify with. While everyone should have the right to use the restroom they want to—and despite legislative victories in recent years regarding restroom usage—many transgender individuals still face both verbal and physical harassment simply for using the restroom.

Gender-neutral restrooms are a great way to dramatically increase people's bathroom safety. If a restroom is not divided into "men's" and "women's" facilities, nobody using that restroom would go in with stereotypical expectations about who else should be in there or how they should look. If stalls were made higher

Restrooms. It's an issue of safety and comfort, whether one is cisgender or transgender. *Refuge Restrooms* is a mapping project for finding gender-neutral bathrooms accessible to the public, with the goal of providing a place of refuge in "times of need." www.refugerestrooms.org

(and lower, or completely encased), identities would be protected. This would improve the whole restroom experience for all—those who are transgender and those who identify all along the spectrum, including parents with children and disabled people with differently gendered assistants or family members. It also would help to cut down unequal bathroom waiting lines.[71]

ACTION STEPS

In addition to exploring resources such as the aforementioned and *These Are Our Bodies* age-level programs, there are many simple actions churches can take to help minister to all of its members (Christ's body).

- Churches can provide changing stations in every restroom, can provide family restrooms, and can provide genderless restrooms, especially for single-stall restrooms.
- Websites, social media, and signage should show the diversity of individuals, couples, and families.
- References should be made to children and adults, rather than girls/boys and men/women.
- Use names on mailing labels rather than Mr./Mrs./Ms.
- Make sure any forms you use do not use male or female "boxes" for checking off one's gender; make sure your forms are open ended with a place for one to write in their own preference.
- Organize directories by multiple last names, co-listing couples and families under names of multiple heads of household.
- Have openly LGBTQ+ individuals serve in leadership positions such as on vestry, at the altar, teaching Sunday school, or serving as youth mentors each suited to best using their spiritual gifts.
- Use inclusive language during worship.
- Examine where you have outreach ministries and with whom you collaborate for interfaith events.

> **The Center for Lesbian & Gay Studies in Religion and Ministry** has developed a well-crafted plan that helps churches and communities begin the work of lovingly preparing for people to express their true selves. http://clgs.org.

Marvin Ellison reminds us that in order for Christianity to remain a dynamic, living tradition, one that addresses real life in a constructive manner, our theological insight and ethical wisdom must adapt and change. "We find continuity with the tradition whenever we join our forebears in faith by making our own spirited commitment to seek justice, compassion, and mutual respect alongside one other and in relation to the earth."[72]

In our churches and communities of faith, embracing these new concepts and vocabulary will help people to talk about their sexuality and express a deep part of themselves.

A love that stems from the God who is love (1 John 4:8) infuses the heart of the Christian message itself: "A God who, through the incarnation, life, death, resurrection, and ascension of Jesus Christ, has dissolved the boundaries between death and life, time and eternity, and the human and the divine." This same love, in turn can challenge and open up preconceived, binary understanding of sexuality and of gender identity.[73]

When we give a name and a voice to the experience in our lives, we are able to seek understanding and move the needle of acceptance toward a full embrace and celebration of all people. We are all created in the image of God to love and honor one another.

Discussion Questions:

1. What is your understanding or belief regarding the *Imago Dei* (image of God)?

2. What is your reaction to the Genderbread Person image? Where do you see yourself in this image? Do you follow the socially defined roles and behaviors assigned to your gender?
3. What challenges you in this chapter? What more do you need to explore?
4. How has your church prepared to welcome people who identify as transgender (or gay, lesbian, bi-sexual, . . .) in your congregation? How can you, personally, prepare?

CHAPTER 7

CARE FOR THE BODY

From the time we are babies we are taught how to care for our bodies: how to keep our bodies clean and healthy inside and out, how to deploy our bodies into the world, and how to keep our bodies safe and protected. All of these aspects of caring for the body are connected to each other. How we care for our physical self affects how we feel about and care for our psychological self, which affects how we care for our spiritual self. All parts of our bio-psychosocial and spiritual self are connected to all the other parts. The health of one affects the health of another.

Care of the body is not a task of simply caring for our skin or external parts. It is much deeper than that, yet there are basic needs at each level that must be met. All of these aspects also provide an expression about ourselves to the world, explaining how we feel and experience the world around us.

BASIC NEEDS

Bathing, eating, sleeping, and exercise are all critical aspects to caring for the body and "the sexual body does not exist apart from the body that eats and drinks, bathes and dresses, rests and exercises, and works."[74] The human body is designed for movement and activity. Physical activity has many benefits. It supports our internal systems. It can help reduce stress and depression, our risk of heart disease and stroke, and can make us physically stronger by improving muscle tone and flexibility. Additionally, study after study has shown that exercise and regular physical activity improves brain health, memory, and thinking skills.[75]

Food and sleep help our bodies recover from physical activity and fuel our bodies for all that we do. Sleep provides time for our bodies to recover and heal from physical demands of the day. It also provides time for our brains to process events, experiences, and materials we are learning. Getting enough sleep at the appropriate time of day for each person's age is crucial to our health. For example, babies need sleep during the day to help them sleep at night. Understanding sleep hygiene can help you sleep better at night and be more alert during the daytime. As we become more and more technologically connected, it is becoming more important to unplug from our digital devices before heading to bed as the light from the electronics stimulates the brain.[76]

Food not only provides energy and essential nutrients to keep our bodies running, strong, and healthy; meals provide a wonderful way for people to connect to one another. Couples, parents and children, and friends can work together to prepare a meal in the kitchen, providing a place for teamwork and collaboration. Meals provide a space for people to sit together in community and share

Examples of **good sleep hygiene** include avoiding napping during the day, avoiding stimulants such as caffeine, nicotine, and alcohol too close to bedtime, establishing a relaxing bedtime routine, and making sure you receive exposure to natural light during the day.[77]

about their lives. Each Sunday in The Episcopal Church we take time to recount the meal Jesus had with the disciples by breaking bread and blessing wine in remembrance of Jesus. Think of all the ways your church and/or family spend time together around a meal.

Water is also an essential part of our lives; without water there is no life. Water is a powerful force included in many stories of our faith. As Christians we are welcomed into the community through baptism when we are washed in holy waters. Bathing is an important part of caring for the body. Metaphorically we can bathe in the sound of the lapping waves of the ocean, a babbling brook, or rain falling. These are sounds that many people use to help restore their spirit, relax, or even fall asleep. Washing our bodies helps to wash away germs and dirt from the day. A hot shower can be relaxing. A morning shower can be a reviving start to our day.

Caring for the body can be a demanding task. It takes focus every day to eat enough vegetables (at least three servings a day), drink enough water (half your body weight in ounces of water every day), and to get enough physical activity (at least thirty minutes a day). Finding support through family, friends, church, and your community helps to make this easier.

A HOLY TASK

Our faith tradition models how we can care for the body. Jesus's actions and teaching show a regard for the body and the holiness of caring for our body, mind, and soul. Jesus took time to pray with his disciples and time to be alone to renew his body and spirit. After a particularly demanding time of ministry, after he had seen the great need in the town, Jesus left the next morning without ministering further to the people in the town.[78] Jesus ate with the marginalized, his disciples, and friends.

One of the most sacred things that we do as Christians is to celebrate the Eucharist: "In Holy Eucharist the worshipping community offers its life, individually and together, to God."[79] In the Eucharist we are compelled to remember. The word "remember" means to re-member. When we re-member, we re-join the Body of Christ. A spiritual meal is at the heart of our Christian practice—sacramentally feeding our bodies as well as our souls.

Jesus also responded to people by providing the most basic necessities. He responded to the needs of others when he turned barrels of water into wine and loosened the law to allow gleaning on the Sabbath. "The goodness of Jesus Christ, the revelation of God, was offered to the world in a human body. His body was an expression of deep goodness, and he used his body to care for the bodies of others."[80]

We can emulate Jesus in the way he showed the importance of caring for our bodies. Maintaining a healthy body is countercultural in our media-saturated world. Our children understand at an early age that our bodies must look a certain way—they should embody the "standard" of perfection at any given moment. This can be seen in highly sexualized cartoon characters and pop stars that often serve as role models. Body materialism can be just as harmful as materialism for "stuff." Despite what our society teaches us about our bodies through magazine articles and television advertisements that focus on "perfect" physical appearances, we know that we are made in God's image and loved for who we are, not what we are.

BODY IMAGE

But all is not an uphill battle. Several corporations now offer a new vision of beauty, especially for girls. The *Dove Campaign for Real Beauty*[81] was launched in 2004, featuring advertisements, video, workshops, and more that aim to celebrate the natural physical variation embodied by all women. Its goal is to help women and girls have the confidence to be comfortable with themselves as they are.

Recently France (joining similar policies in Italy, Spain, and Israel) has banned "excessively thin" models and now requires digitally altered images be labeled as "touched up."[82] Anorexia is a driving force behind these laws. Up to 30 million people of all ages and

> **Integrity** is a personal quality of being honest and having strong moral principles. Holy Scripture tells us what is good and what the Lord requires of us: to do justice, embrace faithful love, and walk humbly with [your] God. Micah 6:8

genders suffer from an eating disorder (anorexia, bulimia, and binge eating disorder).[83]

The Christian practice of honoring the body is born of the confidence that our bodies are made in the image of God's own goodness. Paul writes to the Corinthians, "Don't you know that your body is a temple of the Holy Spirit who is in you? Don't you know that you have the Holy Spirit from God, and you don't belong to yourselves? You have been bought and paid for, honor God with your body."[84] Living into our baptismal promises as people of God, our spiritual integrity is also expressed in our care for the body.

Discussion Questions:

1. How do you care for your body? How are you modeling this to others?
2. Where does prayer fit into your life? How is your body a temple of the Holy Spirit?
3. Which of the biblical stories shared most resonates with you (Mark 1:32–39 or Mark 2:22–28)? Is there another biblical account that you can also share that speaks of caring for one's body, mind, or spirit?
4. What is your definition of beauty?
5. How do your children observe you caring for your body that might impact their understanding of sexuality as they grow and mature?

CHAPTER 8

RESPONSIBLE BEHAVIOR AND DECISION-MAKING

Thinking about the complexities of our human sexuality can be overwhelming, not only in terms of our own expression of our sexuality but in the implications for our own behavior. How then are we called to live a faith-filled life while honoring our bodies and ourselves?

When we move closest to whom God has created us to be, we lean into our best selves: the best self that is made in the image of God, the self that does not need to show off or draw attention to us. Our true self is integrally connected to our soul. When we consider each of these aspects of ourselves, we can live a holy life seeking Christ in others. How can we choose to live in relationship with others in a way that causes our soul to sing? In a world where the traditional moral boundaries seem outdated, where can we look to find a compass, a true path that can grow with us?

WARNING SIGNS

The ways that we are learning and growing into ourselves is changing. In the recent past, children and young people learned to navigate their world in small ways. They learned to ride their bike in the driveway and then down the street. They learned how to cross the street, taking notice of cars. The sidewalks and stop signs provide a warning that a greater level of risk and danger is ahead. Warning signs give us time to shift gears to consider new information. That new information may lead us to turn back or to continue on, knowing that we are safe. Either way, warning signs give us a way to keep ourselves safe and help us to make more-informed decisions.

This process of graduated skills gave developing children and teens some natural warning signs to help learn accountability and responsibility. Our academic system, sports world, and even our library system have ways to say, "Stop. There is danger ahead." Our movie-rating model gives people the tools they need to discern the level of possible risk. To a ten-year-old who seeks to watch a PG-13 movie, the rating says, "*Wait*, be warned, what you are about to experience comes with more complexity than you might realize." The warning doesn't ensure the ten-year-old will not see the content in the PG-13 film, but it does warn parents and children that the outcome might not be good. The same goes for adults who seek to avoid excess language or violence in movies. The ratings give people a way of estimating the danger.

Another way to learn safe behavior is to experience rules and norms that are transparent. The academic and sports worlds give good examples of expected behavior and the consequences when ignored: plagiarism and cheating, rules around sportsmanlike conduct. A standard is applied, in part, to help us make choices that benefit both the community and the individual. "Codes of Conduct" and group norms provide necessary boundaries and help us to be our best selves out in the world.

As children, teens, and young adults enter into new situations, the desire for independence is countered by risk. The progressive stages of boundary making are tested alongside increasing independence and responsibility. Boundaries, warning signs, and accountability standards create a system that both teaches and encourages sound decision-making. As in all stages of our lives, this includes our sexual behavior—toward ourselves, as well as others:

- Respect peoples' opinions, beliefs, experiences, and differing points of view.
- Respect everyone's identity and background, including pronouns and names. Do not assume anyone's gender identity, sexual preference, survivor status, economic status, background, or health status.

In terms of sexuality, those warning signs and boundaries might be the threat of embarrassment or risk of "getting a reputation." The gossip that might ensue after a night of poor choices could be an effective warning sign that the behavior had gone too far. Fortunately, the nature of old-fashioned gossip, before enhanced communication via technology, was limited to a fairly small social circle and short lived. Gossip would eventually become stale and old and the gossiper would be forced to the next new juicy story. The whole affair could be learned from and left behind. That is not the case today.

The Mazzoni Center of Philadelphia offers a Trans Health Conference every year. They offer this **Code of Conduct** to all who participate:

- Respect everyone's physical and emotional boundaries. Check in before discussing topics that may be triggering (such as sexual abuse, physical violence, or encounters with the police), and use a trigger warning during presentations and events.
- Be responsible for your own actions; be aware that your actions have an effect on others, despite what your intentions may be. Listen and change your behavior if someone tells you that you are making them uncomfortable.
- Be aware of your prejudices and privileges and the space you take up during the gathering.[85]

BALANCING RISK AND FREEDOMS

In our modern world those systems that gradually allowed for more freedom while mitigating risk and imposing accountability, can be overused, lacking, or completely absent. The expression of sexuality is one of the areas where the traditional warning signs, boundaries, and accountability are ineffective in our modern world. Short-lived gossip has been replaced by permanent videos and instant pictures. A night of small-town risk-taking, like flirting or going home with someone, could potentially be visible to hundreds of social network connections, forever.

Expressions of sexuality are no longer contained in a relatively small social system. Expressions such as dress, hair, dancing, and flirting are witnessed by those who are not actually anywhere near the experience. The consequences of behavior are often more damaging as the "hook up" or sexual expression is posted for public viewing on social media or YouTube. The healthy embarrassment—feeling that you did something wrong—is replaced with public shaming. Feeling that you are bad, rather than feeling like you made poor decisions, rips at a person's core with messages that say (sometimes literally), "You are worthless." Our electronic world of smartphones and continuous connectivity creates play spaces that lack both the warning signs and natural limits that would introduce incremental freedoms and responsibilities.

If the new goal is to gain attention and acquire "likes," then the pressure to explore is boundless. In the past, to flirt, dance, and be noticed would require people to go into public. Flirting, dancing, and attention seeking can now happen in the privacy of a bedroom

Questions to think about: Even the concept of online friends is confusing. How can you be friends with someone you do not know? What if we called those onlookers voyeurs? How can you learn to be a friend when you have hundreds of friends and the pressure is on to "get as many likes as possible" on social media?

or bathroom. In those private spaces, where technology enables strangers to view our lives, the natural warning signs are missing. There are not friends telling you to stop. There is not a delay before the pictures are developed. And now we have an immediate way to objectively quantify how much attention is gained.

THE OPEN STYLE PLAYGROUND

The online availability of pornography is a good example of an open play space that lacks warning signs or boundaries. Within a few seconds anyone who can type and click can stumble onto pornography sites. Porn advertisements are "pushed" into browsers. You do not even have to go looking to find porn—it finds you.

The area of active media, where we upload and download, is another space where we lack the normal warning signs or transparent, clear guidelines that give us a chance to pause to consider the landscape ahead. Our open style playground of electronic connectivity, says, "Come, play, record, share, everything is fair game." And too often young people respond with expressions of sexuality that seem out of character. The most well-behaved teens post centerfold pictures or forward explicit pictures within seconds of receiving them. And the community wonders, "How did this happen?" In the open style playground, the consequences are delayed, if there are any. And the call to be provocative and relevant within online social networks provides the space for mistakes that are recorded and permanent.

The online world can beckon and shout: "Try this. Do this. It is fun." Although being connected electronically seems to provide real connection, the connection is often far from true intimacy and relationship. The online personas that people create can be places of emptiness posing as real relationship. In the realm of online profile making—an environment detached from community, connectedness, and intimacy—people are more likely to make risky decisions, leading people to experiment more boldly with relationships and sexuality. Young people are making decisions about

Sexting is sending and receiving sexually explicit messages, primarily between mobile phones. Once an adult practice, it is increasingly used by middle school and high school students.

sexual expression in an environment where they can be duped into behavior that is damaging to them and others. This atmosphere of "anything goes" leaves us wondering, how can we offer some useful guidance on sexual behavior for these online environments? What do we have to say about the new ways of expressing ourselves virtually?

Our new connectivity is here to stay. There is no wishing it away or going back to the good old days of phones that are attached to the wall. With every new technology, we have to grow into the new play space. By developing conventions and habits that help us navigate the new space, we claim it as our own and eventually impose some boundaries and warning signs that help us learn to manage freedom. What new boundaries are being created? How are we regulating our play space to stay safe and to help us grow into our very best selves?

MAPPING NEW PATHS

In the Search Institute's newest study of developmental relationships, the researchers found that the quality of the parent-child relationship is more than ten times as influential in the development of "critical character strengths" as demographic factors such as community and peer group affiliations.[86] For example, children ages three to thirteen must learn to navigate school and life despite their demographic markers (income, family structure, ethnicity, and race). Some of those necessary skills are strengthened through stronger parent-child relationships including "being motivated to learn, being responsible, and caring for others."[87]

One key to mapping out a new path involves sacred spaces where children and adults can talk about their lives and what is most important to them. By developing safe harbors (our families, churches, and communities), we provide essential places for the conversations that matter—vital conversations that can lay seeds that can be transformational.

What do those conversations look like? They are free of judgment. They are free of dogma and shame. They recognize and model that we all step beyond the path and even decide to take an unknown path every now and then. We can ask questions that help people see their choices in a new light. These sacred spaces are where we can ask:

- What is challenging right now?
- When you are falling asleep at night, what are you thinking about?
- If you could picture three months from now, what do you want to wake up thinking about?
- What are your conversations looking like with your brother, sister, parents, closest friend, and/or partner?
- If someone picked up your phone and posted your normal day, what feeling would that evoke? What would you be proud of? What would cause you embarrassment?

We can wonder how we can . . .

- ask questions that lead us to look to the future;
- ask questions that invite us to reflect on our behavior;
- ask questions that help us affirm people;
- ask questions that create boundaries;
- say, we love you, you are loved by God, fully completely— just as you are.

We can say, if you are feeling uncomfortable, you can tell us that. You can change the behavior. You can ask for help. You can cry. You are loved every day and every moment.

FALSE NARRATIVES

When our sexuality begins to take hold of us and seems to be out of control, we move away from being balanced in our body, soul, and mind. Our balance is off-kilter as our identity becomes wrapped up in our sexuality and behavior. People might justify their behavior with "anything goes if it isn't hurting me." Why is this line of thinking a problem? Because our values shape our behavior and our behavior shapes our self-identity. Our behaviors define how we view ourselves and, in turn, how we transmit that identity to others. Our behavior shapes and reflects who we think we are, whether that is a positive or negative thing, or something in between. And who we are matters. Our self-identity matters because the messages we tell ourselves are important. When we see our bodies and sexuality as disposable aspects of ourselves, we are in danger of living out the definition of that new identity, believing that we are unworthy. Once we see that others see us as unworthy, our identity and our self-perception begins to change. What we do, think, and how we behave are matters of substance because they shape and define how we see ourselves.

The "anything goes" culture teaches that our own pleasure and satisfaction are at the center of our identity and that we can sacrifice or suppress our values and emotions to see that our needs are met. That false narrative can create a life that separates emotions from actions. When we behave as if our feelings and emotions are not important, we lose the grounding knowledge that we are "made in the image of God" and live, instead, as if we were made in the image of ourselves. We disconnect our emotional and spiritual lives from our actions: Rather than growing more into the best person we can be, we move farther away from that very best self. Integration of our whole being (body, mind, and soul) is a goal of spiritual maturity; moving away from that integration creates disconnection, isolation, and pain. We forget who we are. We cannot hear God's loving whisper, "You are my child with whom I am well pleased." We lose our way.

SOME QUESTIONS TO ASK

Being lost is not new to Christians. We are experts at losing our way and straying from the path. It is part of being human. When lost, the

New Testament gives us ample hope in trusting in Jesus, who declares himself the shepherd who knows each sheep in his flock. "I am the good shepherd. I know my own sheep and they know me."[88] We can also lean on the knowledge that the Kingdom of God is like the widow who lost the one precious coin and searched for it until it was found.[89] God continues to whisper to each of us. The call to follow is always there. The church community is a safe place to land for re-direction and comfort, with a few lighted pathways to make the coming home easier without the shame or judgment that is the cornerstone culture's narrative.

What can be our guideline to shape our moral ground, if guilt and threat are not the mainstays of a life providing morality? Living into the dream that God has for us—in the fullness of a life lived as body, soul, and mind—requires new ways of being and new methods of self-examination.

A way to conform to situations and norms that we have not yet envisioned is to enter into discernment. Strict rules and "can and cannot do" scales leave us struggling to find a sense of boundaries and right and wrong within a changing world.

We are called to ethical responsibility that encompasses an inherent lack of selfishness or exploitation. The gospel calls us to a life of responsibility: a place where we can accept the consequences of our choices without guilt or blame. Much of our society models a life lived to satisfy only ourselves, while Jesus's life and teaching call us to live lives that are sacrificial and at best reject selfish, narcissistic behavior as alien to a holy life.

Exploitation is another warning sign that can help steer our choices and behavior toward right and holy relationships. If we are behaving in a way that takes advantage of someone's innocence, position, or body, we can name that as exploitation. Could we be called to a better life by asking of ourselves each time before we make a behavior choice:

- Is it irresponsible?
- Is it selfish?
- Is it exploitative?

The questions that we ask ourselves help to ground us in the invitation to live a life worthy of our calling. We can ask ourselves, "Is this moving me closer to my true self? closer to my best self?"

"Our sexual relationships are meant to be occasions of joy—moments when we discover again the richness of the life-giving meeting with the person we love. And more, our sexual encounters can be moments when our physical and emotional connections with a beloved human being can open our eyes and our hearts to the expression and the promise of our loving relationship with almighty God."[90]

Discussion Questions:

1. What helps you determine your moral compass?
2. In what ways has a "code of conduct" changed in the public sphere, through the sports, entertainment, academic, or political arenas? Has this impacted you in any way?
3. How has the Internet changed your "code of conduct" in the social media world? How has this impacted (or not) your behavior or that of others that you know?
4. Where are your sacred places and safe harbors? What qualities make them sacred and safe? Where do you go for discernment?

CHAPTER 9

CONSENT AND SHAME

While we tend to believe that adolescence is a time of growth and discovery, we should acknowledge that each one of us, regardless of age, is constantly learning more about our bodies as well as building new relationships with others. Knowing ourselves and listening to the desires of others can help us distinguish between healthy and unhealthy behaviors; understanding the difference helps us develop healthy attitudes and behaviors, which creates positive opportunities for learning. We are then also equipped to intervene when we have concerns about unhealthy behavior, poor self-image, or sexual violence.

Knowing ourselves is impactful in our relationships with others as well as with ourselves. Stephanie Paulsell speaks to this:

> We cannot respond to another's bodily needs and desires with compassion unless we have the capacity to imagine those needs and desires. But even though our bodies are distinct from the bodies of those closest to us, it is through our bodies that we are also able to enter into relationship with others.[91]

CONSENT

Understanding the complexities of consent in sexual relationships must be taught to each generation. Thanks in part to heightened attention to student safety on college campuses, the topics of consent and responsibility are widely discussed these days. But consent and responsibility are not issues of importance only for college students. Teens, young adults, and older adults all struggle with issues surrounding consent. Responsibility and consent are relevant for many aspects of life—not just sex. For example, we talk about making safer choices all the time by teaching people (adults and kids alike) the importance of responsible gun ownership. We try to educate ourselves on the responsible thing to do if people are being physically abused. Conversations about consent, responsibility, and respecting another person as a beloved child of God are crucial for healthy relationships.

The basics of consent are simple. Consent is more than not saying "no." Consent is saying "yes." Teaching that "no" means "no" to each new generation is key. Anything unclear means "no." Anytime someone is too incapacitated to give a clear, talked-about audible "yes," it means "no." The only thing that means "yes" is a clear, audible, talked-about "yes" that is freely given without repercussions for saying "no." Additionally, either partner can change their mind at any time. Simply because a partner has previously consented and participated in sexual activity at any level does not mean they must participate in said activity the next time. Consent works both ways; both partners have the right to consent or not.

From the Faith Trust Institute: "**Consent** is about having the capacity and the real option to say 'yes' or 'no' to someone else's sexual initiative. If you say 'no,' you shouldn't be punished. If you're punished for saying no, it's the same as saying 'you can't say 'no.' That's not a choice, and that's not consent."[92]

There are cultural issues that create problems for mutual consent. "In the dominant culture, sex is imagined as an unequal social exchange between a social superior and a social inferior. It ceases to be about love or the sharing of mutual pleasure between willing partners. The traditional Christian sexual ethic is implicated in this mess because it has legitimated a moral code of male entitlement over women and female bodies. The implication is that good sex is when a man uses a woman for procreation and bad sex is when a man uses a woman only for pleasure.[93]

"As long as men as a social group retain disproportionate power and as long as prevailing institutional arrangements reinforce male privilege and status, then the problem of male violence against women, children, and less powerful men will not disappear. Sexist cultural norms and values support notions of male superiority and the right to rule over and discipline others, a prerogative that some men play out violently."[94] However, this is not entirely an issue of male dominance over women, children, and less powerful men. Research indicates that abuse occurs at the same rate in gay and lesbian relationships as it does in heterosexual unions and, further, that same-sex victims suffer the same types of abuse as heterosexual women endure at the hands of their batterers, including physical, emotional, psychological, and sexual violence.[95]

Consent is about mutuality and a willingness to care for your partner—regardless of gender—to mirror back the image of God that exists in each person. We have a responsibility to help transform our religion into a "more fully humanizing and egalitarian faith tradition."[96] What does it mean that God named all creation "good"? What does it mean that God was made present in the body of a human being? "Our faith can help us if we pay attention to how God's love of difference is expressed in the many different bodies that grace the earth and how God's care for us is expressed in the sexual intimacy that our God-given bodies make possible."[97]

We must stop shaming and fear-mongering so all people feel safe and free to give consent when they want to without repercussions of shame or guilt. We must stop teaching people that sex is a commodity to be bartered or manipulated away. We must help and support each other when someone is violated, raped, and/ or physically assaulted. It is never the fault of the person who is hurt—NEVER. Help them seek support from a professional and keep their story confidential, as it is their story to tell.

THE PURITY ETHIC AND SHAMING

Related, but at the opposite end of the spectrum, are those who have been taught not to give away their virginity or even their sexuality. This creates a sense of shame around embracing sexuality and expressing it. Unmarried girls and women are coached in the purity ethic that holds virginity as the greatest and most precious gift that they must protect above all over virtues. This purity myth teaches that sexuality is to "be given" to a man in marriage and rejects the natural expression of desire. Women are judged as promiscuous for wanting to kiss, pet, or have sex with someone.

A different ethic or standard applies to men. Too often, men are tacitly taught to "sow their wild oats" and that violence or irresponsibility is forgivable and necessary growing pains for men. This stud-versus-slut dynamic teaches a false narrative for both men and women. It keeps women in the shame-based sexuality model and clouds men's ideas about sexuality: Men want women to be interested in sex; but if the woman is interested, she is considered a slut.

Jessica Valenti begins her book *The Purity Myth* by pondering the problems with defining virginity. In fact, there is no medical definition for virginity. Dictionaries do have definitions for virginity, however, most definitions are female focused; there are no definitions that are specifically male focused. Virginity used to be a commodity. "Now, instead of women's virginity being explicitly bought and sold with dowries and business deals, it's being defined as little more than a stand-in for actual morality."[98] The implicit and sometimes explicit message is that sex, at least non-heterosexual and/or outside of marriage, is shameful, makes a woman (or gay man) less worthy, and immoral.

> **Slut-shaming** is a form of social stigma applied to people, especially women and girls, who are perceived to violate traditional expectations for sexual behaviors.

Abstinence-only education is part of the problem in the advance of the purity ethic. Abstinence-only education is heterosexually focused, discriminating against all other types of relationships. Perhaps now that same-sex marriage is legal in all fifty states, this will begin to change. Regardless, abstinence-only education does not teach participants about contraception options and oftentimes provides inaccurate and misleading information.[99]

Culturally we must stop slut-shaming women (and men for that matter) and stop telling men they must "man up," perpetuating some false sense of machismo. We should be teaching men and women to embrace their sexuality, their sexual desire, and to have conversations with their partners. Everyone evolves into relationships at different paces. It is important to have conversations with your partner about what you are reaching for. We must come to a place in society that makes it safe for people to be ready (or not ready) for kissing, sex, or anything in between.

The reality is most Americans have premarital sex. "In fact, by the age of forty-four, 99 percent of Americans will have had sex, and 95 percent of us will have had sex before marriage."[100] Instead of focusing on a false sense of purity and creating unnecessary shame, we should focus on teaching people how to properly use a condom and educate about other contraceptives. Sexual fidelity, mutual vulnerability, and responsibility are behaviors we should strive to instill. We should focus on helping people develop healthy relationships rather than alienating people because of their sexuality.

It is important to support healthy attitudes and behaviors for our own sakes, but also for those for whom we serve as models and mentors. We should speak up when we hear of abuse in any form, support those who have been violated, and report such incidences to the proper authorities when required by law. Respecting the dignity of all and advocating for justice is rooted in our baptism.

Discussion Questions:

1. Have you ever been "shamed" for something? How did it make you feel? How did you respond?
2. How do you define "consent"?
3. How do you define "purity"?
4. What place has consent and/or purity played in your life? Has your understanding changed over time? Why or why not?

CHAPTER 10

CHANGES IN CULTURE

Culture is constantly shifting and changing. We have made much progress as a society. Looking back, some of these societal changes are apparent. The birthrate, death rate, and the average age for marriage and death have all shifted in the United States. Media, technology, and improvements in medicine are just a few examples that shape the ethos of society, and these specifically (among others) have impacted our views on sexuality.

In a 2015 study (*What Americans Believe About Sex*[101]), Barna Group surveyed 1,000 American adults about their thoughts on sex. When asked about the purpose of sex, the most common answers given were "to express intimacy between two people who love each other (63%), to reproduce/to have children (60%), and to connect with another person in an enjoyable way (45%)." However, disparities were noted between generational cohorts, with Elders and Baby Boomers supporting more traditional views while only one-third of younger generations (Gen-Xers and Millennials) believe sex should unite a man and a woman in marriage. Millennials are much more likely than older adults to say the purpose of sex is self-expression and personal fulfillment (40%).

Barna Group editor-in-chief Roxanne Stone stated that the research shows the collision of new and old attitudes about sex in society today. "The big story here is how little everyone agrees on when it comes to the purpose of sex. This current lack of consensus points to a growing ambiguity and tension over its place in society and in the individual's life." She added, "Sex has become less a function of procreation or an expression of intimacy and more of personal experience. To have sex is increasingly seen as a pleasurable and important element in the journey toward self-fulfillment."

A NEW SEXUAL ETHIC

Today's culture is inundated by messages of sex, technology, convenience, and a sense of immediacy. We are still feeling the effects of the 2008 stock market and housing market crash. Many people are in massive amounts of debt; unemployment and job replacement is slow to recover; and many have not seen a pay raise in years despite increasing costs of goods and services. Pharmaceutical companies seem to have developed a medication for anything that ails us. Many families are overextended as they try to "keep up with the Joneses." In one of his meditations, Richard Rohr ruminates on how letting go is countercultural. "In a consumer society most of us have had no training in [letting go]. Rather, more is supposed to be better."[102]

All of these changes in culture shape our relationships, sense of self, and sexuality. For the last decade several people, such as Marvin Ellison, Margaret Farley, William Loader, and Timothy Sedgwick, have written about a need for new sexual ethics in general and specifically for singles. Our culture is changing; how we choose to live out our faith and invite others into it, along with our sense of ethics, must be responsive to it.

In *Sex God: Exploring the Endless Connections Between Sexuality and Spirituality*, Rob Bell talks about the importance of a trophy he had as a child that he still has an adult despite the damaged state of the award. To Bell, the trophy is more than a trophy. His story illustrates how we hold onto items "because they point beyond themselves, to something of more meaning. This physical thing—this picture, trophy, artifact, gift—is actually about that relationship, that truth, that reality, that moment in time."[103] He goes on to list a variety of things that are actually about something more than what they are and that these "things" are connected to our sexuality. "It's always about something else. Something deeper. Something behind it all. You can't talk about sexuality without talking about how we are made. And that will inevitably lead you to who made us. At some point you have to talk about God."[104] Bell is correct; we must talk about God, about how we are made. We must also understand the shifts in culture. Bell discusses the shift in family structure:

> Part of the problem arises from the human tendency to assume that what is at this moment has always been. We hear about the 'traditional family' in which the father worked, and the mother took care of the children, who went to school, played, became adults, and married. The truth is that such a family configuration is from a post-Industrial Revolution time. Prior to industrialization, everyone in the family worked except the small infants, and even into the nineteenth century, six-year-olds labored for twelve hours a day at the looms of northern England. Because circumstances have arisen in Western society that may be calling for different responses to life than those made by our parents, we need to be sensitive to our place in history and evaluate our responses in light of this time and place and the contemporary human condition.[105]

THE CHANGING LANDSCAPE OF MARRIAGE

The "institution" of marriage has significantly changed over the last several decades. While divorce rates have slowed—nearly two-thirds of marriages will *not* end in divorce—more people are delaying marriage or remaining unmarried. Twenty percent of people over the age of twenty-five are unmarried which is up by 9 percent since the 1960s. There are many reasons for this delay: changes in gender roles, modern marriage is more about love than survival or financial stability, and more men now remain unmarried than women. As more women are educated and enter the workforce, marriage becomes less and less about survival. Due to many factors such as the shift in gender roles and the poorer job economy, financial stability is becoming a prerequisite to marriage rather than marriage being a stepping-stone to financial stability. This shift in the idea of marriage is one of the many reasons there is a need for a new sexual ethic.

Same-sex marriage is now legal in all fifty states. In 2015 the General Convention of The Episcopal Church approved same-sex blessing and marriage rites. This societal shift is affecting the shape of religion and vice versa. These kinds of changes will continue to occur as each generation ages. Millennials (even among traditionally conservative groups such as evangelicals and Mormons) are more accepting of same-sex relationships than older generations. "Fully half of Millennials who identify as evangelical Protestants now say homosexuality should be accepted by society."[106]

"FAMILY" IS CHANGING

The *New York Times* issue of "Science Times" offered a series on "The Changing American Family"[107] in 2013, offering a changing definition of what the American family looks like today. Norman Rockwell's family looking on with glee at the Thanksgiving Day turkey is no longer the norm; researchers have expressed their astonishment at how rapidly the family has changed in recent years. Fewer women are becoming mothers, and those who do are having fewer children. More than 40 percent of American babies are now born to unmarried women, mostly women in their twenties and early thirties. Families are more ethnically, racially, and religiously diverse than half a generation ago.

There has been a rise in single people who happily live alone. And growing numbers of same-sex couples are pursuing parenthood through adoption and surrogacy, creating a new kind of baby boom for gay parents.

The American Academy of Pediatrics states in the February 2002 edition of its journal that children raised in a homoparental environment develop just as well as those raised in a heteroparental environment. It also concludes that children would benefit from having both of their same-sex parents legally recognized, encouraging legislators to take the necessary action to make this possible. The legalization of same-sex marriage allows the structure for same-sex parents to be recorded as co-parenting. Some simple changes on student and parent forms (using terms such as parent one and parent two instead of Mother and Father) open the door to the normalization of same-sex parenting. The American Psychiatric Association takes the same position.[108]

How one might meet one's life partner has also changed. Online dating services are booming. And once that love connection has been made, many choose to cohabitate without walking down the aisle. However, those who do choose to marry are waiting; marriage has become an act of later adulthood, thus increasing the number of births to unmarried parents.

Each of these family configurations exists in our congregations. The shifting of societal norms, changing family structures, and our cultural expectations all have an impact on how we live as sexual beings in responsible ways. And these shifts point more to the need for faith communities to support its members of all ages in learning how to live a whole and healthy life, following our baptismal promises.

Discussion Questions:

1. How would you define your sexual ethics?
2. Do you agree or disagree with other generations (younger or older) about premarital sexual relationships?

3. What is your definition of "marriage"? Has this changed in recent times or remained the same. Why or why not?
4. What does "family" mean to you? What has your experience of "family" been throughout your life? How are you similar or different from your grandparents in your understanding of what constitutes a family?
5. What do you believe the qualifications should be to be a parent? Where do those personal ideals come from?

CHAPTER 11

BEYOND STEREOTYPES

Most of us have felt the painful experience of being stereotyped—judged by a few characteristics to be exclusively part of one group. Although we know that pain, we continue to paint people with the brush of judgment and narrow thinking.

Stereotyping is a way to judge others without the risk of seeking to understand. Stereotypes help people to lazily assess others without the burden or discomfort of getting to know individuals. One of the dangers inherent in stereotyping is falsely judging what makes me different from you, makes me better than you. Stereotyping keeps us from seeing people as individuals and hinders our capacity to embrace people who are different from us. When we can see the differences and uniqueness in others without judgment, we move toward celebration of all people. That movement helps to spread *agape* love—the love that lets be. This love does not minimize differences; it recognizes our differences, lifts them up as beautiful, and inspires us to seek connection.

SEXUAL STEREOTYPING

In the arena of sexuality, automatic stereotyping and judging can strain and break our relationships with others without our even recognizing the pain we are causing. The words we use, the stories we tell, and the jokes that propel our conversation often alienate others who have a different life experience. Practicing awareness and mindfulness in our relationships moves us toward a grace-filled life that makes room for people with a variety of backgrounds, experiences, and identities.

Teaching children about stereotypes and exploring with them the depth of pain that they can inflict on others when they make rough judgments about people is essential. Teasing, name-calling, and harassing others make most adults wince; yet, this bullying behavior is still commonplace in our schools and churches. Teaching children and teens to recognize stereotyping and helping them find healthy ways to respond in groups empowers children and teens to live a life that brings their faith into their everyday lives.

The goal of loving and understanding one another continues into adulthood as we seek to accept all people. In our modern world where diversity is valued, our ability to love and understand others may be tested. Often, as people grow spiritually, they are challenged by their own set of preconceived ideas—even judgments. These judgments are often statements that seem, to us, to be neutral and inoffensive. We may casually ask if someone has children, if they have a boyfriend or girlfriend, or when they plan on getting married. Those questions make assumptions about the lives of the people

The Mazzoni Center defines **oppressive behavior** as any conduct that demeans, marginalizes, rejects, threatens, or harms anyone on the basis of ability, activist experience, age, cultural background, education, ethnicity, gender, immigration status, language, nationality, physical appearance, race, religion, self-expression, and/or sexual orientation.[109]

Some tips for empowerment:

- You do not have to go along with people who are name-calling or mocking others.
- Standing up for a friend or acquaintance can be as simple as standing next to the person being harassed.
- Standing next to someone who is being bullied gives that person strength and lets them know that they are not alone.
- Have practice conversations or role-play with other group facilitators, your partner, your co-parent, children, and teens.
- Teach children to smile at people instead of staring, laughing, or pointing.
- Begin to pay attention to those who most people don't see. Often people serving or cleaning are "invisible." As followers of Christ we aim to "respect the dignity of all people." A simple "hello" or "thank you" can have ripples of positive goodwill.

around us. Instead of being open expressions of interest, they seem inconsiderate or hostile to someone who is not dating or struggling with infertility.

Most often it is people who are close to us who can help us see our offensive language and stereotyping. A friend can help us see that minimizing anyone's struggles—with weight or mental health, for example—can be painful to others. The same is true for sexual identity.

A FEW HINTS FOR OPEN CONVERSATION

- Make statements in conversation instead of questions. Say, "I would love to know more about you." "Please tell me more about that." "I can't wait to hear what you are passionate about these days." Those statements allow others to control the topic of conversation.

The **GLAAD** website has a chart of words to avoid and words to use for download.[110]

- Avoid assumptions around gender. "Who is your boyfriend?" "Are you still dating her?" "She is so pretty." Choose more fluid language, "Tell me about your friends." "You are energetic and interesting."
- Just ask. If you are unsure of a term or a phrase, just ask if you are using the correct term. "Am I saying that correctly?" "Am I using the best word?"
- Assume good intent: Whether you are struggling to adopt new terminology or you are leading others to new ways of thinking, assume that people have the best of intentions. Irritation and judgment only increase stereotypes instead of opening them up. Crediting people with goodwill and treating them with kindness is our way of being the hands and feet of Christ in the world.

BULLYING

Habits of stereotyping fuel judgment and violence. Adults too often excuse bullying as a normal and unavoidable behavior of children and teens. The platitudes of "children will be children" are unhelpful and dangerous. Bullying is often dismissed as being the victim's fault, or with the encouragement that bullied children will grow emotionally or build character. Bullying is a systemic issue that deserves our intentional response and care.

For LGBTQ+ persons, the added pressure, stress, and pain of ridicule and humiliation are a growing concern. Studies show that between 1 in 4 and 1 in 3 students between sixth and eighth grade experience bullying.[111] The inability to accept the differences in another person's gender, identity, or expression can be the catalyst

> **How do we become more neighborly** and encourage mutual respect with those who may identify differently than we do? First, we must understand who we are as an individual, an image of God that is loved for our own uniqueness. To understand who we are is to lay a foundation to grow into the full stature of Christ.

for bullying. How can we advocate for the right of all people to be treated equally and fairly?

In our spiritual life, judging can make us blind to our own shortcomings and masks the universal call to love and forgive. Love is illuminating whereas judgment is alienating. Jesus asks, "Why do you see the splinter that's in your brother's or sister's eye, but don't notice the log in your own eye? How can you say to your brother or sister, 'Let me take the splinter out of your eye,' when there's a log in your eye? You deceive yourself! First take the log out of your eye, and then you'll see clearly to take the splinter out of your brother's or sister's eye."[112]

Somehow judgment satisfies a need to be better than others, which is in direct opposition to the assertion that we are all created in the image of God. Judgment is a form of objectification. As an object, the person is viewed stereotypically—in a narrow, confining view. Judging blinds us to the individuality and humanness of others. In judging we use the difference between two people as the evidence that one person is somehow better than another. Love is the antidote to judgment and stereotyping.

LISTENING

Katharine Jefferts Schori, twenty-sixth Presiding Bishop of The Episcopal Church, sees listening as a key component to understanding and reconciling love. Preaching in St. George's Cathedral, Jerusalem, in January 2015 she said, "Listening deeply to the story another person tells is an essential and holy way of opening that space. What does that require of us? Slowing down, sitting down in patience, breathing

Suggestions to further the conversation:
- Role-play bullying scenarios to build empathy.
- Make time for intentional conversations.
- Listen to the stories that others tell.
- Teach and model respect for the dignity of all people.
- Work for equality and fairness for all people, including the LGBTQ+ community.
- Model acceptance.
- Examine your own perspective and hidden judgments.

deeply, and focusing our attention on another rather than ourselves. It is a kind of prayer, listening for the creative word of God in another. It is a conscious act of loving our neighbor as ourselves."[113]

As followers of Christ we are called to respond with love, rejecting the temptation to belittle and criticize. What if we sought to see the uniqueness and differences in others as opportunities for understanding and reasons to celebrate?

The Gay, Lesbian and Straight Education Network offer these suggestions:

10 WAYS TO BE AN ALLY[114]

1. Don't laugh. Let others know that jokes and comments based on race, religion, sexual orientation, gender, ethnicity, etc., are not funny.
2. Speak up! If you feel safe, let those who behave disrespectfully know that you don't appreciate it.
3. Challenge bystanders. If you feel safe, let spectators know they are not helping.
4. Don't "Get even." Responding to meanness with meanness won't help matters.
5. Be a friend. Show kindness and support to the targets of negative behavior.

6. Involve adults. Tell a teacher or counselor about ongoing incidents and get support at home from parents and family members.
7. Be nonjudgmental. Demonstrate to others that you are willing to listen and talk with an open mind.
8. Be inclusive. Ensure that your language and behavior are respectful to all people.
9. Be self-reflective. Be aware of your own prejudices and work to change them.
10. Take action! Speak out against bias in your community and in the media.

Discussion Questions:

1. Have you ever been stereotyped? Share an example. How did it make you feel?
2. Have you ever bullied someone in any shape or form? What led you to that behavior and how did it make you feel?
3. What has been a "splinter in your eye" regarding the sexuality of someone else who is different from you?
4. Where have you seen pain caused by bullying or stereotyping another human being? Where have you seen redemption in such cases?
5. What do your children observe you listening to (music, radio, talk shows, recorded books) or watching (televisions shows or movies) that might impact their understanding of sexuality and stereotyping?

CHAPTER 12

SEXUALITY EDUCATION FOR ADULTS

Adults should not be exempt from sexuality education. The "Chastity/ Purity" model and the "Abstinence Only" model, while dated, are still a strong part of our culture, utilized in schools and churches. These old examples do more harm than good in that they do not recognize people as the embodied spirits and spirited bodies they are. These practices focus on ignoring or putting out the fire of desire that is a natural part of being a sexual being. Outdated educational models focus only on young people and do not teach safety, while excluding adults and many college-age people from the conversation. There are, however, a variety of reasons to offer sexuality education for adults.

ACTIVE ELDERS

An estimated 80 percent of fifty- to ninety-year-olds is sexually active. The number of cases of syphilis, chlamydia, and gonorrhea among forty-five to sixty-four-year-olds in the United States and United Kingdom has risen.[115] There are a number of reasons attributed to the rise of

STIs in this older population. People are living longer and new trends in medicine have provided medications for erectile dysfunction and female lubrication. More older adults are dating and do not necessarily perceive themselves at risk.[116] Given that three quarters of Episcopal congregations consist of at least 50 percent of people over the age of fifty,[117] we can assume many of these "statistics" are people in our pews.

Older generations are helping to raise and educate younger generations—supporting them through the stumbling stones of aging, yet the older generations are still learning. The Church must continue to provide support in the form of education and information for adults so they may better lead youth. It is important that we talk about topics such as living in a Viagra® world. What message is conveyed to people when more and more medications are available to help women experiencing low sexual desire or suffering from post-menopausal issues, and men suffering from erectile dysfunction? Is the message that aging as a sexual being is abnormal or bad?

> "**Erotic desire:** seeks physical, emotional, and spiritual embrace of others, the world, and God, the sacred source of life."[118]

Eroticism is the creative power within each of us. "Our sexuality involves far more than merely genital aspects; it is the wellspring of that *eros*, that passionate drive that is the source of art, creativity, and work well done, the source of making music and pleasure, as well as for sacrament and mutual caring. We must not forget that the great power of our sexuality can be used as an instrument of our destruction as well as a source of our joy. Our sexuality, apart from God, can give rise to jealousy and strife, to manipulations and exploitation, dividing and alienating us just as surely as it can bring us together."[119]

EDUCATION IS NEEDED

Adults can discuss a wide array of topics around sexuality and the body. Groups can discuss concepts that may be new to them such as gender identity versus gender expression, and sexual orientation versus romantic attraction. Organizations like Planned Parenthood offer programs on topics such as sexual pleasure, aging and sex, general sex education, and communication and sex. Providing educational opportunities with a registered nurse or an organization like Planned Parenthood can help improve adults' knowledge about contraception and safer sex with regard to STIs.

Marvin Ellison writes about the complicated ethics of sex and having a partner with Alzheimer's.[120] Stephanie Paulsell writes beautifully about honoring the suffering body and the importance of caring for those who are aging and/or ill.[121] Additionally, churches can provide space for adults to explore the sexual ethics of single adults as well as that of older, coupled adults.

Throughout history, many teachers have recognized there are stages to human and spiritual growth and development. "They all affirm that growth and development have a direction and are not a static 'grit your teeth and bear it.' Unless you can chart and encourage both movement and direction, you have no way to name maturity or immaturity."[122] It is through the wider perspective of the later stages of life that you can understand the earlier stages of life.

Elders are an essential part of the church; with the wisdom and leadership of adults in the second half of life, the church can continue to deepen its faith. Our sexuality remains with us our entire lives. As our bodies age and our life circumstances change, our need to continue learning about our bodies—our spirituality as well as physical and emotional being—never goes away.

Discussion Questions:

1. What are ways that you, as an adult, can continue to learn about your own sexuality in the context of your faith and life?
2. What does it mean to be a mature person?
3. What does "living in a Viagra® world" mean to you?
4. How do you define "erotic"?
5. How will you remain a sexual being as you age? What are the implications of your thoughts, feelings, and actions regarding sexuality?

PART III

THE BIOLOGICAL

For Young Persons

God our Father, you see your children growing up in an unsteady and confusing world: Show them that your ways give more life than the ways of the world, and that following you is better than chasing after selfish goals. Help them to take failure, not as a measure of their worth, but as a chance for a new start. Give them strength to hold their faith in you, and to keep alive their joy in your creation; through Jesus Christ our Lord. *Amen*.

—BCP, p. 829

CHAPTER 13

PARENTING AND HEALTHY DEVELOPMENT

The best gift a parent can give a child in the arena of sexuality is a parent who is comfortable with their own body and can model a healthy view of sexuality. Learning to love our bodies can sometimes take years, but it is never too late to enjoy a better self-image. As adults we also need reminding that we are made in the image of God. Our whole selves, body and soul, are created to love God, one another, and ourselves. Modeling that self-love and acceptance translates into healthy habits and perceptions in our children. Being comfortable in our skins allows parents to teach children healthy self-talk and self-perception.

Children are experts in mirroring behavior that they observe. A family that openly enjoys physical activity will most likely raise a child who is drawn to an active lifestyle. A child who sees adults who hide their sexuality will be less willing to express their own sexuality. This chapter, and the ensuing ones, offers a brushstroke on human development. How we grow physically, morally, and cognitively impacts our sexual development and offers insights into how we can provide our children information that is developmentally appropriate as they grow.

WHOLENESS VS. SHAME

Healthy sexuality begins with accepting ourselves and learning to befriend ourselves. Parker Palmer writes about the quest for wholeness in *Let Your Life Speak*. "An inevitable though often ignored dimension of the quest for wholeness is that we must embrace what we dislike or find shameful about ourselves as well as what we are confident and proud of."[123] Parents who do the reflective work of understanding their bodies, souls, and minds integrate their lives to model wholeness to their children. Parents teach and model love for others by caring for their young children. We learn to love by being loved, and by loving.

> "**Wholeness of life** is given first of all in the family, to the extent that these first, most intimate relations of life are not means of securing a haven but invite us, rather, to embrace and care for the other as other."
> Timothy F. Sedgwick[124]

Parents begin teaching their children about bodies from the first moment that they hold their children. Most parents do not intentionally consider the lessons they are teaching their children as they hold, feed, and caress their infants and young children. A gentle touch or a hurried, rushed touch teaches either kindness or frustration. The words used at changing time echo in children. When a bowel movement is met with "That is stinky, YUCK!" it teaches a toddler that their bodily functions are inherently revolting and creates a sense of shame. According to Brené Brown, "Shame is the intensely painful feeling or experience of believing that we are flawed and therefore unworthy of love and belonging."[125] Shaming is unhealthy and emotionally painful. Parents can substitute empowering words of affirmation and acceptance that can work to create shame resilience in their children.

A more affirmative choice would be, "Let's get you cleaned up and more comfortable." Leaning into the infant or toddler to blow on their stomach playfully demonstrates connection. That intimacy and tenderness says: "You are worthy. You are loved. You are treasured." And those messages of love and acceptance are felt through their bodies; they are the messages of meaning. Children who feel loved— body and soul—grow up with a sense of worthiness and belonging.

Children are a gift to families—and families are charged with bringing up healthy children who have a positive view of sexuality. To foster healthy sexual education at home, families can create loving and supportive relationships, while teaching responsibility for self and others, and valuing equality in sexual identity, attraction, and expression.

HUMAN DEVELOPMENT

As an adult, it can be easy to forget what it was like to be a child or adolescent. We often forget that each age and stage of our lives provides opportunities for embracing our sexuality. Most parents have not been trained in human development, so the following chapters provide a general overview for each stage of development. These milestones are helpful to keep in mind when determining what, when, and how we talk about sexuality at each age and stage.

Our faith development occurs concurrently with our other development, influenced by the interplay of many internal and external forces including: biological maturation, emotional and cognitive development, social interactions, religious symbols, religious practices, and cultural norms and values. In 1981 James Fowler's groundbreaking book *Stages of Faith: The Psychology of Human Development and the Quest for Meaning* (New York: Harper

> **"Child development** is an interdisciplinary field devoted to the study of human constancy and change from conception through adolescence. It is part of a larger discipline known as developmental psychology, or human development, which includes the entire lifespan. Child development research has been stimulated by both scientific curiosity and social pressures to better the lives of children."[126]

Collins, 1981) hit the shelves. Fowler continued, along with many other faith development theorists, to push our understanding of how our faith develops *and* that it develops in combination with all other developmental aspects of our lives.

While we are simultaneously teaching children and adolescents about their body, we are also shaping their moral, faith, and meaning-making development. We will begin with cognitive development, while reviewing moral and faith development in the next two chapters. Although this is an umbrella term that incorporates many different fields, the individual fields of psychology can seem dissimilar to each other. Even when the different areas of developmental psychology have similar goals, there is no theory that is 100 percent accepted.

A HIERARCHY OF NEEDS

Abraham Maslow (1908–1970) worked in the area of motivation and developed a therapeutic technique called self-actualization and a theory of progressive psychological needs that requires that each stepped level of needs must be satisfied before moving on to the next level. Maslow's hierarchy of needs is commonly used today to understand human development through the lifespan. This framework demonstrates understanding how our human needs must be met in order to progress to the next level from the basic (physiological) up to the highest (self-actualization). Maslow's hierarchy of needs is frequently displayed in a pyramid with five needs from the base to the top.

Maslow's Hierarchy of Needs[127]

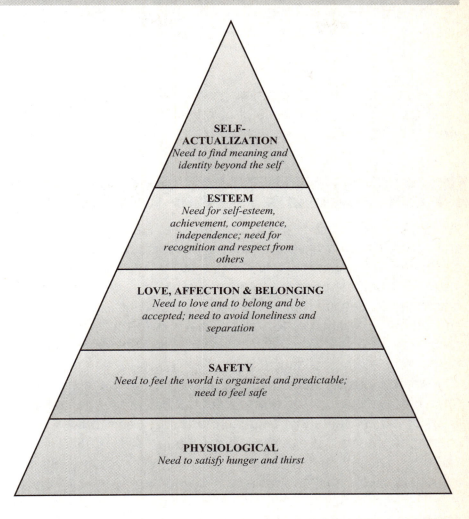

SELF-ACTUALIZATION
Need to find meaning and identity beyond the self

ESTEEM
Need for self-esteem, achievement, competence, independence; need for recognition and respect from others

LOVE, AFFECTION & BELONGING
Need to love and to belong and be accepted; need to avoid loneliness and separation

SAFETY
Need to feel the world is organized and predictable; need to feel safe

PHYSIOLOGICAL
Need to satisfy hunger and thirst

Applications of Maslow's needs are imbedded in our understanding of how children learn new information. As parents and educators, our first imperative is to provide a safe place for children to express themselves. Often within the church we talk about needing a sense of belonging and how that need to feel part of a group, to be accepted and loved, is a primary motivator for our participation at church. Maslow's hierarchy of needs shows the importance of framing our

Developmental psychology is the blanket term for the study of how humans, children and adults, as individuals and as a group develop physically, cognitively, and socially over time.[128]

worship, teaching, and programming with a system and a culture that develops and sustains a sense of belonging for our young people to grow and thrive within our churches.

DEVELOPMENTAL THEORIES

In addition to Maslow, psychologists Jean Piaget, Lev Vygotsky, and Albert Bandura have contributed substantially to the theories of human development. Jean Piaget (1896–1980) posited in his stage theory that humans move through four stages of cognitive development: Sensori-motor, Pre-Operational, Concrete Operational, and Formal Operational. The stages have definite beginnings and endpoints, and adults should assist a child in development by using the Socratic method of questions.[129]

Applications for Piaget's theory are broad within teaching in the Church as well as how we teach about our bodies and our sexuality. Many of the concepts that we teach to children and to adolescents change as the child progresses through these stages. Bible stories and the questions that we pose to six-years-olds produce different responses than with youth who are well into their teen years.

Children in their pre-operational years love to pretend play and can envision themselves in the biblical stories, yet are limited by their concrete thinking. To better reach them during these years, we translate the stories of our faith into narratives that younger children can understand or learn through play. During our teenage years, we can more readily use the abstract reasoning and exploration of metaphor to apply faith to our lives; we also experience interpersonal relationships at a deeper level. Adult leaders can muse with adolescents about the wilderness times in their lives—plus the times

Jean Piaget's Four Stages:[130]

Sensori-Motor:
Experience the world through the senses (looking, hearing, feeling, touching) and through actions (mouthing and grasping).
- Birth to 2 years
- Uses senses and motor skills
- Items known by use
- Object permanence learned
- Stranger anxiety

Pre-Operational:
Too young to perform mental tasks. Represent things with their use or images; using intuitive rather than logical reasoning.[131]
- 2–6 or 7 years
- Pretend play
- Language used
- Egocentric thinking

Concrete Operational:
At this stage, children grasp both transformations in math and the theory of conservation.
- 7–11 years old
- Mathematical transformations
- Logic applied, has objective interpretations
- Conservation (mass, volume, number, ideas, classifications remain the same despite the changes in the appearance of the objects)

Formal Operational:
Reasoning moves from the wholly concrete thinking to encompass abstract thinking.
- 12 years to adulthood
- Thinks abstractly
- Capable of hypothetical ideas (broader issues)
- Ethics, politics, social/moral issues explored

of angst in the wilderness of puberty—and the metaphorical manna that brings unexpected provision into their lives.

Piaget's work informs our own experiences and ministry by urging us to ask, "Are children developmentally ready to learn this?" Although Piaget's work is still influential today, human development is now understood on a continuum, thanks to discoveries made about learning at younger ages. It was his research on the impact of the first two years of life, however, that spurred further research on Piaget's theories.

Lev Vygotsky (1896–1934), a Russian psychologist, built on Piaget's theories on child development—putting forth his own theories on the effects of social influence and interaction on child development.[132] Vygotsky, working in the twentieth century, asserted that child development was affected by the child's culture. The Zone of Proximal Development is defined by "the distance between the actual developmental level as determined by independent problem solving and the level of potential development as determined through problem solving under adult guidance, or in collaboration with more capable peers."[133] This theory explained the difference in development in children from varying cultures. His concept of the Zone of Proximal Development theorized that learning and knowledge were not only reliant on previous learning but also influenced by culture, peers, and adult guidance. Children were not static in their abilities or skills; on the contrary, children learned from the society and culture surrounding them through direct and indirect learning.[134]

A child's culture plays a large role in their development. One implication of Vygotsky's theory posits that adults should work to ensure that a culture of support, responsibility, and encouragement are maintained as a child grows and learns.[135] Language, as a primary social interaction, plays a role in social mentoring. As a result of Vygotsky's social theory, we see that "by mentoring children and giving them new words, parents and others provide a temporary scaffold from which children can step into higher levels of thinking."[136] This includes their understanding of their own sexual development.

Albert Bandura (1925–) built on Piaget's theories of cognitive psychology by developing his theories of social psychology—namely the idea that children learn things because of a natural progression, not just as result of reward or punishment. You learn just by seeing it, not because you are rewarded. The four processes of Attention, Retention, Production, and Motivation explain that children develop and change with age. Therefore, the age of the child affects social learning.[137] This supports the belief that sexuality education should begin at an early age, building upon children's physical as well as emotional development.

Erik Erikson (1902–1994) was a German-born analyst whose eight stages describe how children progress through each stage sequentially to the next stage. He drew a clear picture of which type of learning is the focus during each stage. In Erikson's model a primary conflict or "psychosocial crisis" is defined as a conflict that stimulates growth and development. The more success the person has in navigating the crisis at each stage, the greater the individual's likelihood of experiencing healthy development in the future. It is interesting to apply this theory to the opportunities we're given to grow in understanding of our sexuality in a healthy (or unhealthy) way.

Much of our understanding of the primary task of children and young adults originates from Erikson's theories. The conventional wisdom to not do things for children that they can do themselves flows from Erikson's *Autonomy versus Shame* stage. It is during this stage when children need to gain a sense of autonomy and accomplishment in doing the tasks that they can be successful doing

Albert Bandura's Four Processes:[138]

1. Attention: Children gradually improve in their ability to pay attention.
2. Retention: Children gradually improve their ability to remember things they have seen or experienced.
3. Production: Children's abilities gradually improve.
4. Motivation: Motivation changes as children get older.

Erik Erikson's Eight Stages:[139]

1. *Trust vs. Mistrust* (from birth to 12 months):
When this stage is successful, infants form loving and stable relationships that build a foundation for later stages.

2. *Autonomy vs. Shame* (1–3 years):
Infants and toddlers assert their independence as they navigate the world around them. They exercise their will and do things for themselves to build a sense of autonomy, rather than shame.

3. *Initiative vs. Guilt* (3–6 years):
Preschoolers learn to initiate tasks, and to make and carry out plans. They practice showing inventiveness as their environment presents novel experiences and challenges. Children might develop guilt if their independent behavior is too demanding, aggressive, or careless.

4. *Industry vs. Inferiority* (6–12 years):
The elementary-aged child learns to be industrious as they learn a whole host of new skills, especially at school. Children learn the pleasure of applying themselves to the task at hand or they feel "inferior" to others that can show itself as a feeling of uselessness or failure.

5. *Identity vs. Role Confusion* (12–18 years):
The main task of this adolescent stage is developing a sense of self, an identity. Teenagers work to refine their sense of self in terms of their opinions, tastes, interests, occupation, sexuality, and preferences. Teens work to integrate that sense of self by testing roles and then integrating those roles into a more developed identity. The risk of not successfully navigating this stage includes a confusion of self-identity, over identification with peers, or confusion over sexuality.

6. *Intimacy vs. Isolation* (young adulthood 20s–40s):
The primary charge at this developmental stage is for individuals to form close relationships that exhibit the capacity for intimacy and love. If young adults are unable to form healthy and intimate relationships they risk social and emotional isolation.

7. *Generativity vs. Stagnation* (middle adulthood 40s–60s):
Generativity means giving to the next generation through child rearing, caring for stagnation of other people, or productive work. The person who fails in these ways feels an absence of meaningful accomplishment."[140] In middle age, people seek to make a meaningful contribution to society through work and family.

8. *Integrity vs. Despair* (late adulthood 60s and up):
People in this stage look back on their lives and feel either a sense of success or failure and reflect on what kind of person they have been. Integrity comes from "feeling that life was worth living as it happened."[141] Older people who are dissatisfied with their lives fear death.

with practice. The idea is that we stifle children by coddling them and do them harm by taking over their problems without allowing children to grow their independence. We help children best at this stage when the adults around them encourage their independence and allow them to struggle while at the same time giving them a safe place to learn and grow.

Erikson identifies the middle childhood stage (6–11 years) as *industry versus inferiority*. The child's task is to learn as much as they can and to begin to "do" things well. They begin to feel a sense of satisfaction. Erikson writes, "One might say that personality at the first stage crystallizes around the conviction 'I am what I am given,' and that of the second, 'I am what I will.' The third can be characterized by 'I am what I can imagine I will be.' We must now approach the fourth: 'I am what I learn.'[142]

The developmental work of adolescence and the teenage years is what Erikson describes as *identity versus confusion*. His research and theory informs our understanding that the adolescents in youth programs are busy developing, forming, and testing their identities. They are deciding who they want to be and how that identity fits within the larger world. One of the most important roles that the church can provide adolescents is a place to try out their ideas, their dreams, their sense of right and wrong, and a safe place that will catch them and hold them when the world rejects them.

Providing that accepting place of love and nurturing is key in our ministry to youth. As they grow and test their sense of self, faith, and meaning, we can remind them that they are God's precious children—beloved and accepted. We can provide a stable place for them to struggle with the key questions of adolescence:

- Who am I as an individual?
- What do I want to do with my life?
- What values should I live by?
- What do I believe in?[143]

Discussion Questions:

1. Are you comfortable with your body around your children? How do you model this?
2. How do you experience shame? How is this different than guilt? Do you have any memories of shame or guilt related to your sexuality? If so, where do you think they came from?
3. What does your child need from you as their parent in order to develop a healthy relationship with their bodies?
4. What portions of the developmental theories examined in this chapter resonate with you in watching your children grow and develop? Which ones do you disagree with?
5. How can these theories help you in teaching your child about human sexuality and their own body?

CHAPTER 14

MORAL IDENTITY

For us to make meaning we must engage our mind. We are hardwired to make meaning by our creator. The human brain seems to be biologically driven to ask challenging questions and seek challenging answers. Interestingly, the prefrontal cortex, an area of the brain responsible for judgment and insight, is also one of the regions of the brain made active during religious experiences, which may partially account for adolescents' intensified search for meaning.[144] Around the time of puberty, this area of the brain has a growth spurt, and continues to develop into our mid-twenties. Our sense of right and wrong derives from our biological need to connect to others, and our moral behavior develops in relationships as much as it comes from rules. "Our moral sense is an integral part of our personhood. An important implication is that the moral needs of children are not merely personal and private. They are also social and shared. They are needs that, in a good society, will command that attention and resources of the community as a whole."[145]

> **Meaning-making** is the defining of a concept or experience outside of oneself. **Moral identity** is about the importance of moral ideals, traits, and actions to a person's sense of identity.

Meaning-making and the formation of a moral identity are ongoing processes. As we develop from childhood through teenage years into adulthood, developing cognitive abilities and expanding social networks provide opportunity to discern new sources of meaning-making. The process occurs whether we want it to or not and can happen in a good or bad way.

Furthermore, the prefrontal cortex, an area of the brain critical for judgment and insight, does not fully develop until around age twenty-five; therefore young age groups lack the capacity to make critical judgments about their own behavior. Adolescents seek out adventure, novelty, and risk, which may be attributed to a "reward deficiency" stemming from altered levels of dopamine in the young, adolescent brain.[146] With the onset of puberty, tweens, children who are not young children anymore and not yet teens, are flooded by hormones creating physical and emotional desire long before they are capable of making critical judgments of how to use their bodies. Often tweens and teens are left without the direction and support they need to discern which behaviors are dangerous and which are merely experimental. The Church must take these findings into consideration when discussing moral issues of our bodies and taking responsibility for doing what is right and pleasurable.[147]

MORAL REASONING

Lawrence Kohlberg (1927–1987), sought to describe the ways human beings think about what is right or wrong. His research led him to posit that humans develop intellectually through three levels and six stages of moral thinking.

Kohlberg's Three Basic Levels of Moral Reasoning:[148]

Level 1: Preconventional Reasoning
This first level is typically before age nine, when the morality of children is focused on their individual self-interest. Children obey rules in order to gain rewards or avoid punishment.

Stage 1: Punishment/obedience. Whatever leads to punishment is wrong.

Stage 2: Rewards. The right way to behave is the way that is rewarded. "What will I get if I do this?"

Level 2: Conventional Reasoning
In this level, a person first makes decisions to gain approval, and later in response to law or out of a sense of duty.

Stage 3: Good Intentions. Behaving in ways that conform to "good behavior."

Stage 4: Obedience to authority. Importance of "doing one's duty."

Level 3: Postconventional Reasoning
Moral reasoning is guided by community versus individual rights, and later by universal principles of ethics.

Stage 5: Difference between moral and legal right. Recognition that rules should sometimes be broken.

Stage 6: Individual principles of conscience. Take account of likely views of everyone affected by a moral decision.[149]

It is important to highlight that Kohlberg's stages are about justification for decision-making and moral judgment, not about the reasoning process that brought people to a certain conclusion or about personal behaviors and actions. Participants in Kohlberg's research were given a dilemma and asked to make a judgment about a character's actions. Kohlberg was most interested in why the subject came to their conclusion rather than the process that led to that decision. Although Kohlberg's theory focuses on the justification for a certain action, the theory supposes that a person's moral reasoning would be more responsible, predictable, and consistent the higher a person scores on the scale.

In recent years, Kohlberg's theory has lost significance due primarily to Piaget's developmental stages becoming less relevant.[150] Kohlberg's theory was also linked to moral philosophy and thus limited the inclusion of the moral cognition and ethical theories. Lapsley and Narvaez put forth that "social cognitive theory has resources for conceptualizing the facts and details of human nature in a way that promotes the construction of powerful, integrative moral theory."[151]

Lapley and Narvaez continue in their discussion of the need to bring cognitive psychology to moral psychology.

> The metaphor of vision seems particularly helpful in coming to grips with what it means to be a moral person. It has been said, 'What we *see* depends on who we *are*.' That is, our appraisal of the moral landscape, our moral vision and our very ability to even notice dilemmas depend on our character.[152]

We know that humans develop and change in response to their culture and to their environment. As examined here, research in the area of child moral development has expanded to include the practical side of moral development. How can parents and teachers encourage, guide, and teach children about moral development? Researcher Marvin Berkowitz, a professor of psychology at Marquette University, published relevant research on the topic of moral development in children. Instead of focusing on stages of moral development, Berkowitz described the "moral agents of functioning."[153] The moral agents were the ideas and skills that facilitated moral action. The focus was on the identification of "how parents can be taught to nurture the development of 'building blocks' of morality, a core set of characteristics that either (1) underpin and give rise to moral functioning or (2) reflect fundamental human morality."[154]

MORAL AGENCY

Berkowitz described in "Fostering Goodness: Teaching Parents to Facilitate Children's Moral Development" the parental eight moral agents of moral functioning:[155]
1. Social orientation
2. Self-control
3. Compliance with external standards
4. Self-esteem
5. Empathy
6. Conscience
7. Moral reasoning
8. Altruism

Berkowitz sees these eight moral agencies as the building blocks of moral psychology. The first four are not in themselves moral characteristics; rather as the meta-moral characteristics that provide the framework for the moral self. The last four are the components of moral psychology. These eight moral functions do not arrive spontaneously into our lives at a certain age. Instead, these aspects of a person are integrated into the whole person and cannot be seen as isolated characteristics. Although the four foundations for moral agency, such as social orientation, do not inform moral action directly, each is pivotal in development of the components of "psychological morality."[156] As the foundation for the later four aspects, these foundational components are of special interest in the church where we seek to guide and inform parents over the entire arch of child rearing, including conversations about our bodies and our sexuality.

ATTACHMENT

As social beings, humans are wired for interaction and connection. In this area, social orientation is focused on the attachment of infants and young children from birth to five years old. Attachment refers to the emotional bond or ties to another person and is seen in children when they seek the comfort of the person and show distress when the caregiver or other person leaves.[157] Children who have formed

Five ways parents can aid in the multifaceted transition from impulsivity to self-regulation:
1. Protect children from the effects of their impulsivity by situational management.
2. Provide the ego-controls that children have not yet developed (soothing children during emotional outbursts, for example).
3. Teaching coping skills, like how to shift one's own attention in delay of gratification situations.
4. Helping children to anticipate the consequences of their actions.
5. Modeling self-control.[158]

secure attachments are able to develop the later moral functions of psychological morality with "positive psychological outcomes" that are long-lasting. The characteristics of secure bonding can form the basis for ongoing relationships. Children who do not benefit from successful attachment are at risk of developing antisocial behavior and thought to have more problems developing a conscience.

SELF-CONTROL, COMPLIANCE, AND SELF-ESTEEM

The second characteristic, self-control, is foundational in establishing the delay of gratification, self-discipline, impulse control, and the ability to resist temptation. Berkowitz asserts that individuals "must have some capacity to control their own behavior, such as "the tendency to violate prohibitions while without surveillance . . ., adolescent drug use . . ., self-control in the face of temptation . . ., or empathy."[159]

Nathan Dungan's teaching around money is a textbook example of scaffolding behavior in parenting that yields informed, compassionate, faithful, and thoughtful planning around money. See more at www.sharesavespend.com.

Self-control, as a multifaceted concept, is a learned skill that begins in infancy with toilet training. Parents are able to teach their children self-control by "scaffolding" instruction, guidance, and most importantly the opportunity to practice these skills in a gradual, progressive fashion. Parents provide essential support and continual feedback needed to safely apply still immature skills, which is extremely important as children begin to test and explore their sexual identity.

The third characteristic of moral agency centers on compliance. Parents begin to teach their children to obey the rules imposed by external communities and systems. Sharing is a good example of an external rule of many homes and schools. Children learn to comply with the ground rules that govern their homes, schools, and communities. Wearing a helmet when biking or staying within a certain play area are simple ways that children learn to abide by external regulations.

Parents can build self-esteem by:
1. Accepting their children
2. Setting clear and defined limits
3. Allowing the child's individual expression
4. Respecting the child's unique personality and point of view[160]

The fourth and last of the meta-moral characteristics, self-esteem, is widely recognized as beneficial to the welfare of children. Children who develop strong self-esteem seem to exhibit strong mental health later in life. And although having an exaggerated self-esteem comes with problems of its own, thinking well of oneself is psychologically healthy. This concept of self-esteem is connected to our faith life and our ability to love and care for one another. In our attempts to follow Jesus's second commandment, "You shall love your neighbor as yourself,"[161] we easily stumble when we judge ourselves to be unlovable. Our capacity to love others is constricted by the ability to love and care for ourselves.

EMPATHY AND CONSCIENCE

These four meta-moral characteristics form a foundation for a child's moral capacity that carries into their adult lives. The fifth characteristic, empathy, is a primary emotion needed for morality. Without this ability to see things from another person's viewpoint, the ability to respond with kindness and compassion is necessarily limited. Berkowitz asserts that empathy is learned through modeling. Parents who explain their parenting behavior to the child (especially with a focus on consequences of one's actions for others) have more empathic children.[162]

Conscience "has long been understood as a combination of (1) internalized standards and (2) behavioral and affective results of adherence to or violation of those standards."[163] Researcher Kochanska and her colleagues have explained conscience as having two major aspects:[164] *affective discomfort*, which encompasses the emotional results of transgression (guilt, apology, empathy for the victim) and *active moral regulation* or *vigilance*, which encompasses the classical internalization of standards along with confession, reparation, and monitoring of others' wrongdoing."[165] One key to the conscience is its internalized nature. A person's conscience activates when internal standards are violated. Those internal standards activate the affective discomfort and the moral regulation.

Dr. Brené Brown defines **empathy** as the ability to take the perspective of another person. "Connection is why we're here. We are hardwired to connect with others; it's what gives purpose and meaning to our lives, and without it there is suffering." Her explanation of empathy is delightfully conveyed in this short video. http://brenebrown.com/2013/12/10/rsabear/

PARENTING STYLES

In terms of influence and teaching, parental discipline style and family communication patterns seem to be the most influential in the development of moral reasoning in children. Lawrence Kohlberg has done the most significant research on moral reasoning, with three parenting styles studied:

1. The *authoritarian* parenting style is characterized as being overly controlling and excessively demanding, expecting immediate obedience without discussion or explanation.
2. *Permissive* parents offer firm guidance, but do not enforce boundaries and are overly adaptive to their children.
3. The *authoritative* style, which is neither unbending nor unaware, is the style that was seen to benefit children the most in terms of moral development.

Parents who exhibit an authoritative style were found to be loving, controlling, communicative; they set high maturity demands for their children. According to the researcher Damon, authoritative parenting fosters social sensitivity, self-awareness, and respect for rules and authority.[166] The positive child outcomes, including higher moral reasoning and functioning, were positively impacted by the open, supportive communication style of authoritative parenting. Conversely, Diana Baumrind's work on parenting styles shows that authoritarian parents are overly demanding and controlling in such a way that parents were "affectively cold and hostile and generally uncommunicative."[167]

COMMUNICATION AT HOME

Another aspect of moral reasoning is the impact of open communication, discussion, and conversation in the home. Family discussions of ethics and moral decisions with both parents and children had a positive effect on the child's moral development. Conversations had the most impact when the child's perspective was heard and valued. Parent and child communication had more impact on children's moral development than peer-to-peer conversation. Discussions that incorporate general warmth and support found in the parent and child communications are the most effective, which is in stark contrast to peer conversations that are often characterized by conflict.[168]

ALTRUISM

The fourth moral concept of altruism seems to be one of the most recognized aspects of moral psychology. Parents are integral in the development of altruism in their children. Parents who are able to exercise restraint and avoid overly controlling behavior enable their children to internalize social norms and standards on their own, thereby taking on the rules and standards themselves. In other words, they learn to follow the rules on their own. Sociologists Eisenberg and Mussen concluded that altruistic children tend to be "active, sociable, assertive, advanced in role taking and moral judgment and sympathetic."[169]

The overarching impact of the research suggests that children need to have moral reasoning modeled for them, along with opportunities to discuss behaviors, ethics, and morals. When children see moral reasoning modeled by the adults around them—and when they are given the explanation for behaviors and the values behind those behaviors—they develop and apply those reasoning skills and values in their own lives. Conversations on the overarching values of support, encouragement, and respect are the most nurturing for the child.[170]

When children are raised in a responsive, warm way, they learn that they are valued and worthy of love and belonging: If I am worthy of love and belonging, I can see that others are also worthy of love and belonging. I learn to respond in respect to others in a way that honors their humanity, because I know what it means to be respected. Berkowitz reminds his readers that children experience the best outcomes when children understand their parents' values and the beliefs that inform those values. Parents are integral in shaping the moral development of children.

Altruism is one's selfless concern for the well-being of others. Our baptismal promises can be considered altruistic actions.

In a study published in *Science*,[171] researchers found that, as toddlers, we are approaching the ability to express altruism. In the study, Felix Warneken found that a child as young as fourteen months would help when help was needed. Prior to this study, it was thought that children were born "purely selfish" and become helpful over time through moral education and socialization. "It rather seems to be the case," Warneken writes, "that selfish and altruistic motives are there from the beginning in competition with each other."[172] As a faith community, committed to helping children grow in their moral development, we can continue to teach and guide children in our nurseries as well as our youth groups.

Discussion Questions:

1. How do you understand the difference between meaning-making and moral identity?
2. What are your thoughts about the phrase, "What we *see* depends on who we *are*"? Does this have implications on your parenting style?
3. How can sexuality education help develop one's moral development? one's empathetic ability?
4. How would you characterize your parenting style: authoritarian, permissive, or authoritative, and why? Share some examples. Which do you believe is the best?
5. How do you model moral reasoning to your child?

CHAPTER 15

FAITH DEVELOPMENT

Another area of development affected by our understanding of moral psychology that is central to our conversations about human sexuality in the church community is faith development. James Fowler (1940–2015) contributed to the study of faith development with his books *Stages of Faith* and *Weaving the New Creation* (San Francisco: Harper & Row 1991). Fowler saw faith as a natural and normal part of being human. He did not, however, connect the development of faith with a specifically Christian view.

Fowler's Stages of Faith

Stage 1: Intuitive-Projective Faith (3–7 years old):
A child's first ideas about God are shaped by watching and learning from the adults around them, especially their parents. Children get their first idea of God by attributing the characteristics of the mother or father to God. This way of understanding God is intuitive, not learned. A child's world is filled with imagination and creativity, which can be seen in the way they approach the stories of faith.

Stage 2: Mythic-Literal Faith (8–12 years old):
During this stage, children learn to distinguish between reality and fantasy. In late childhood, when children are venturing farther from their core family and developing the ability for abstract thought, eight- to twelve-year-olds find security in their faith while at the same time vacillating between concrete and abstract thinking. In terms of their beliefs, children at this stage still have a literal understanding of faith and God. For many of them, God is anthropomorphized, thus they understand God as having human form and thought.

Stage 3: Synthetic-Conventional Faith (adolescence):
In Fowler's third stage, individuals are aware of the feelings, beliefs, and attitudes of others and change their own positions, views, and opinions easily. The faith of this stage is not yet fully integrated into adolescents' lives. They struggle with the task of synthesizing their own beliefs with the beliefs of those around them. Synthetic-conventional faith can also be a stage in which many adults find themselves. Adults might see God as a Santa in the sky, a judgmental angry landlord, or a personal guide.

Stage 4: Individuative-Reflective Faith (young adulthood):
As the young person grows and develops a secure personal identity, they begin to have conflict with the values, thoughts,

and attitudes around them. As they move into this stage, young adults begin to take ownership and responsibility for their own perceptions, attitudes, and beliefs. It is individuative in that the faith is a personal one, not adopted or adapted from someone else. It is also reflective in that people in this stage have reflected over time about what they believe and value as individuals. People in this stage are able to engage in rigorous assessment and self-reflection about their core beliefs and values. Thanks to a more developed capacity for abstract thought and reasoning, people in Stage 4 are able to view God abstractly as a spirit and wrestle with moral truths.

Stage 5: Conjunctive Faith (middle life):
In this stage of faith development, adults in middle life reflect on their past and discover influences that have affected their growth and development. Adults in middle life look to their background, culture, and parental, social, ethnic, and religious experience to work through feelings, thoughts, and memories that they may have previously suppressed. In this stage the boundaries that were better defined in Stage 4 are loosened as the adult becomes less rigid and more comfortable with paradox.

Stage 6: Universalizing Faith (later life):
Individuals in this stage have reached the pinnacle of faith development. As a result of earlier personal and spiritual work in the previous stages, a committed individual will work to bring about the universal concepts of love and justice. The level of dedication that people in Stage 6 often exhibit puts them in direct conflict with the political and religious leaders in their time. Martin Luther King Jr., Ghandi, Mother Teresa, Nelson Mandela, and Desmond Tutu are all examples of people who reached this last stage.[173]

John Westerhoff III (1933–) has done seminal work in the area of faith development. In *Will Our Children Have Faith?* he outlines four distinct stages of faith development: experienced, affiliative, searching, and owned.[174] Westerhoff uses the metaphor of a tree to discuss the four stages. Faith develops or grows over time like the rings of a tree, growing an outer ring with each stage. We can visualize how our conversations with children, youth, and adults regarding sexuality might be framed by exploring each of these stages.

John Westerhoff's Styles of Faith

Experienced Faith (preschool and early childhood):
Young children at this stage are experiencing the faith of people around them. They adopt the faith, practices, and beliefs of the people they encounter. A child might learn the Lord's Prayer in that they can recite the prayer, but the prayer does not have personal meaning to the child. It is a faith built around their senses.

Affiliative Faith (childhood and early adolescent years):
In this stage children and teens add another ring to their faith development. They build on the experienced faith that they previously understood. Affiliative children and teens enter into a faith centered on belonging. It is a faith built around their affections and love for being part of something, whether it is a family, youth group, scout troop, or God's Story.

Searching Faith (late adolescence):
When the next ring of faith is added, teens move from a focus on belonging to a stage of searching, questioning, and wondering. This searching faith is an active stage in which adolescents bring

their own reasoning ability into their faith. At this stage, teens do not blindly accept what others are telling them, nor are they content to simply follow along. It is common for teens, during this stage, to actually reject learning from the previous two stages. Teens shun the structured aspects of belief systems in order to build the scaffolding for their own faith.

Owned Faith (early adulthood):
The last faith stage is the outermost and largest ring—as such, it encircles and encompasses all the other tree rings. A person at this stage has been through the years of questioning, debating, and spiritual struggle needed to build a complex, mature faith. This owned faith is a personal and incorporative faith that integrates the experience of personal faith with the rest of a person's life as a whole.

Since Westerhoff first proposed these stages in the 1970s, he has added new insights to his research on faith development. To better understand our faith development, Westerhoff looks to our chronological age, developmental stages, and the characteristics of our life processes and relationships. Using a pilgrimage metaphor for human life, he names three distinct pathways to God. Each leads fully to God; none is superior to the others. These paths, or trails, weave through each other, depending on the choices we make in life. He calls them the *experiential way*, the *reflective way*, and the *integrative way*. From the chronological viewpoint of age, childhood encompasses the experiential way, adolescence the reflective way, and adulthood the integrative way.[175]

As people of faith, we are called to guide our children (and ourselves) in the knowledge and love of God as we grow physically, emotionally, morally, and spiritually. All of our being—body, mind, and soul—is nurtured through ages and stages to the fullness of Christ in a community of faith.

PUTTING IT ALL TOGETHER

We have spent the past few chapters reviewing human development in all its many facets and theories. Human development consists of three main domains: (1) physical, (2) cognitive, and (3) emotional and social. It is important to note that although these three domains are used in development theory, they are not distinct, separate domains. You will see them overlap and intersect.[176] In subsequent chapters we will put all of this together, looking at specific ages and how each of these developmental stages can instruct us and impact us as we learn about our bodies, our sexuality, and our relationships with others.

In addition to differentiating the three domains, researchers also divide time of growth and development into manageable parts:

Periods of Development
- Prenatal (conception to birth)
- Infancy and toddlerhood (from birth–2 years)
- Early childhood (from 2–6 years)
- Middle childhood (6–11 years)
- Adolescence (from 11–18 years)[177]

Domain Definitions from Laura Berk:[178]
- *Physical Development Changes* in body size, proportions, appearance, functioning of body systems, perceptual and motor capacities, and physical health
- *Cognitive Development Changes* in intellectual abilities, including attention, memory, academic and everyday knowledge, problem solving, imagination, creativity, and language
- *Emotional and Social Development Changes* in emotional communication, self-understanding, knowledge about other people, interpersonal skills, friendships, intimate relationships, and moral reasoning and behavior

The next chapters offer a brief outline of the three domains, plus the moral and spiritual realm, for each of the last four periods of development. We will add a separate category for spiritual and moral development. All of these can guide us into developmentally appropriate conversations with our children about sexuality.

Discussion Questions:

1. What is your first memory of God, or the Holy? Where were you? Was anyone with you? Why do you think you remember this as your first?
2. Do you ever question the beliefs of your parents, or your own beliefs? What were the beliefs you questioned and how old were you?
3. Which "ring" of Westerhoff's stages do you feel you fall into right now? Why?
4. As a parent (or teacher), how do you help children grow in their faith?
5. What ways do you model and act out your faith to others?

CHAPTER 16

INFANCY AND TODDLERHOOD

Prenatal care impacts the life that is to come. This nine-month period is the most rapid time of change, during which a one-celled organism is transformed into a human baby with remarkable capacities for adjusting to life in the surrounding world. From birth to two years of age there are dramatic changes in the body and brain that support the emergence of a wide array of motor, perceptual, and intellectual capacities. The beginnings of language appear as well as the first intimate ties to others.

Infants need to be touched and rubbed. All of that skin contact helps their brains develop. Infants soon learn that their bodies feel good. Kissing and play during diaper time begins to teach infants that they do not need to hide or conceal their bodies. Handling any bodily discharge in a neutral emotional state will teach your infant that their body and their discharge are a normal part of life. A boy might touch his penis or a girl might caress her vulva area. Instead of scolding a child, redirect them with play. As people made in the image of God, our bodies are inherently good. Parents who choose to respond in an emotionally neutral way will help their children navigate the complications of sexuality as they grow.

BIRTH TO 11 MONTHS

Physical Development

In the first year, birth weight triples. By three months, infants can support their upper body with arms when lying on stomach; they stretch their legs out and kick when lying on their stomach or back, and can open and close their hands. By six months, infants learn to sit with support of hands and then without hands. At nine months, infants are shaking their head to say "no" and standing by holding onto furniture. They love to play peekaboo. They connect more with people outside of themselves. At this age, babies are putting a few words together. By eleven months, they are able to stand with support. They enjoy dropping and throwing as they begin to grasp cause and effect. Experimenting and playing with food is a way of learning about the world through their senses.

Emotional and Social Development

At two months, infants are alert to people and by three months, develop a smile, enjoy playing, babbling, and responding to a familiar face with a smile. They accept comfort when scared or frustrated. By six months, infants can turn their head toward the speaker and by seven months can respond to their own name. They begin to recognize emotions by the tone of voice—and respond to "No!"

Cognitive Development

- Develops principle of cause and effect
- Learns object permanence
- Communicates with face and body

- Smiles and cries in response to environment
- Works to get objects out of reach
- Makes sounds with voice to express joy and discontent
- Explores by dropping and picking things up
- Curious about their environment

Spiritual and Moral Development

- Develops trust in response to being cared for
- Learns about gentleness
- Seeks to be comforted
- May mimic adults by patting their back when held
- Reaches out with hands to connect with others[179]
- Enjoys physical closeness
- Responds to soothing touch
- Learns fundamental trust in self, caretakers, and environment[180]

Teach Me . . .

- By giving me toys like soft balls, textured toys, and musical toys
- By singing and talking to me
- About the world around me my responding to my babbles
- By playing with me
- About new foods
- By giving me lots of physical stimulation
- By mimicking my sounds
- That books are part of my daily routine

Vocabulary Words to Teach Me

- Infants can learn sign language to help them communicate before they can verbalize all of their words.
- Name of all their body parts including penis and vagina
- Basic feeling words: angry, sad, tired, happy, hungry

12 TO 24 MONTHS

Physical

During this time, birth weight triples. Babies also learn to drink from a cup and pull up to a standing position in their second year of life. Toddlers begin to walk holding onto furniture and explore objects by drumming or shaking. By 24 months, they can kick a ball forward, jump in place, put their clothes on, pedal a tricycle, tower cubes, and wash and dry their own hands. By holding their hands, you encourage toddlers to take steps. They are capable of learning that hitting and biting hurt other people. Redirecting instead of scolding is a best practice.

Emotional and Social Development

- Shy or anxious with strangers, pays increasing attention to speech
- Cries when caregivers leave
- Responds to verbal requests
- Learns to give something to an adult if it doesn't work properly

Cognitive Development

- Uses language to express wants and needs
- Manipulates environment to solve problems (moves a stool or feeds a pet)
- Shows preference to some toys or people
- Repeats sounds or gestures for attention

Spiritual and Moral Development

- Bows head at blessing time or reaches out to hold hands
- Babbles to participate in blessings

- Can put money into the offering plate
- Imitates children and adults
- Is able to get others to take care of them

Teach Me . . .

- How to use my words instead of hitting or biting
- Explain the No's to me
- Tell me stories and read to me
- Sing songs and laugh with me
- About caring for others and encourage empathy
- To share with other people by letting me have a box that is "mine"
- How to wash and dry hands
- Names of body parts
- How to stack blocks
- Words, words, and more words
- How to kick a ball, jump in place, and put on clothes

Vocabulary Words to Teach Me

- My name
- Mom, Dad
- Please, thank you
- Up, down
- Basic clothing: shirt, pants, socks, shoes
- Name of all my body parts including penis and vagina
- Words to express emotions (happy, sad, scared, surprised)
- Words to describe how my body may feel (hungry, tired, hot, cold)
- Naked
- Words for bodily functions: chew, pee, poop, throw up

Discussion Questions:

1. What experience have you had with infants and toddlers?
2. What do you find joyful about this age?
3. What do you find challenging about this age?
4. What have you been told about yourself during this time of your life?

CHAPTER 17

EARLY CHILDHOOD

From two to six years, the body becomes longer and leaner, motor skills are refined, and children become more self-controlled and self-sufficient. Make-believe play blossoms and supports all aspects of psychological development. Thought and language expand at an astounding pace, a sense of morality becomes evident, and children establish ties with peers.

Picture a preschooler dancing and twirling, singing, "Jesus loves me, this I know." That child has internalized the message of God's love of each of us. The child knows what it means to be beloved, to be accepted to their very core. Modeling and teaching that love to children lays the foundation for life filled with wonder; it creates a person who can be comfortable with their sexuality—and it begins in early childhood.

Help children to see their bodies as normal. Parents often wonder when they should start covering up after a shower or dressing with the door closed. Take the clue from your children. When children begin to need more privacy, give it to them.

Showering with children can give them a sense of normalcy around bodies and caring for them. Too often parents pass along their discomfort with their own bodies to their children. They hide in closets to change their clothes; they change outfits looking for something that doesn't make them look fat. Children model what they see. Become a person with a healthy self-image and your child will become comfortable in their own skin.

As children age, continue to play with them in a physical way. Run, jump, and wrestle. Tickle and comfort children with a gentle touch and they will learn that their bodies and the bodies of others need care and love. The way we touch children matters. Children will model our touch as they grow. They can be shown how to meet anger with listening and gentleness rather than a hand raised in violence.

Touch speaks the wordless words of love. We receive so much touch when we are babies and so little when we are adults. Still, in friendship, touch often gives more life than words. A friend's hand stroking our back, a friend's arms resting on our shoulder, a friend's fingers wiping our tears away, a friend's lips kissing our forehead—these bring true consolation. These moments of touch are truly sacred. They restore, they reconcile, they reassure, they forgive, they heal. Everyone who touched Jesus and everyone whom Jesus touched were healed. God's love and power went out from him (see Luke 6:19). When a friend touches us with free, non-possessive love, it is God's incarnate love that touches us and God's power that heals us.

> Henri Nouwen reminds us that a gentle touch or caress can say so much more than words.[181]

PRESCHOOLERS

Physical Development

In the span of two years, young children gain muscle control for toilet training and can walk from heel to toes. Four-year-olds can catch a ball and cut with scissors.

Social and Emotional Development

Preschoolers from two to four years old show more interest in peers and demonstrate more self-control. They communicate their own preferences and develop a greater sense of self.

Cognitive Development

- Thought and language expand
- Learn self-care: dressings, eating, potty training
- Learns colors and to count
- Expands concept of time
- Engages in fantasy play with imagination being a central way to learn
- Views things from one perspective

Spiritual and Moral Development[182]

- Sense of morality is evident
- Children begin to establish ties to peers
- Seeds of faith are sown in these early years
- Learn through imagination
- Responds to concrete images and symbols
- Beginning faith is through imitation
- Feel pride when they are good and embarrassment when they are bad (at 18–36 months)

- Can recognize distress in others, beginning of empathy (at 18–36 months)
- Emotionally attached to toys or objects for security (at 18–36 months)

Teach Me . . .

- To use my words to work through problems
- About friends and to share
- To pick out my clothes and to get dressed
- Tell me stories and listen to my stories
- Introduce me to the larger world around me

KINDERGARTENERS

Physical Development

Five- and six-year-olds love to run, climb, and ride bikes. They enjoy sports and can learn how to swim and other complex physical tasks. Their interest in genital organs is natural and healthy.

Social and Emotional Development

This age can be both cooperative and demanding. They have a greater awareness of sexuality and can show greater independence (or at least a desire for it).

Cognitive Development

- Able to distinguish between fantasy and reality
- Loves to sing, dance, and play
- More likely to obey rules
- Progressively learning to count and color names
- Increase in general knowledge around everyday things (appliances, money, food, schedules)

Spiritual and Moral Development

- Experience joy, love, forgiveness, and grace through the example of parents
- Greater sense of community and friendships
- Can see Jesus as an inspiration for kindness
- Literal and concrete thinkers; they might see God as a miracle worker
- Respond to the narrative of God's people
- Love to learn biblical stories
- May experience death of grandparent or pet

Teach Me . . .

- That no one can touch my genital area (including close friends), except doctors or nurses during an exam, or parents when they are trying to find my source of discomfort
- How to get my needs met if bullied
- My first and last name and my address
- To share and talk about my daily experiences
- To identify my feeling and emotions

Here Are Some Things to Teach Your Preschool Children

- God loves our bodies.
- In the beginning God called everything "very good" (Genesis 1:31).
- God gave us male and female friends.
- Our bodies are beautiful and our parts have names. Teach and review the names of their body parts.[183]
- Name the parts of your child's body that only the child, mommy or daddy, and the doctor may touch. Instruct the child to tell you if someone scares or hurts them.

- Basic concepts of pregnancy and birth including egg, sperm, uterus, how long a pregnancy takes, how the baby is nourished in utero, and how a baby is born.
- Before a child starts kindergarten, make sure he or she knows how a baby gets "in" and "out."

Vocabulary Words (by four or five years old, preschoolers have acquired about 1,500 words;[184] below are a few categories that are important to develop)

- Their first and last name as well as home address
- Name of body parts including genitalia: penis, breast, vulva, vagina
- Self-care words: bathroom, potty, toilet, sleepy, hungry, tired, bowel movement, urinate
- Words to express emotions: happy, sad, scared, surprised
- Words to describe how the body may feel: hot, cold, stinging, burning
- Naked
- Words to use when meeting people: hello, my name is . . ., thank you, no thank you, I am sorry, bye
- Words associated with time: in the morning, before breakfast, after school, before lunch, after play time, non-school day, summer, vacation, break

Discussion Questions:

1. What experience have you had with preschoolers and kindergartners?
2. What do you find joyful about this age?
3. What do you find challenging about this age?
4. What have you been told about yourself during this time of your life?

CHAPTER 18

MIDDLE CHILDHOOD

Younger elementary (6–11 years) children are going to school and spending time away from the home. These years are needed to teach children how their bodies work and how to care for their bodies. Children who learn to bathe and dress themselves learn the importance of self-care that will last them a lifetime.

Teach children that their bodies belong to them. Make sure they know that their kisses and hugs are freely given. Avoid compelling a child to hug or kiss a relative—or anyone else! You will want your child to know that no one can touch their bodies without their permission. Helping early elementary-aged children own their own bodies lays the foundation for healthy boundaries.

In middle childhood, their world enlarges and deepens. Children begin to develop independence and take on more responsibility. They practice the tasks that resemble adult tasks and master some of the basic chores performed throughout life. Children become better communicators and can navigate the school environment. They learn to gather their things and to bring them home. They master basic academic skills like literacy, writing, and basic math concepts.

In the later years of middle childhood (between 8 and 11 years old), although they still value parents and family, independence from their family becomes more important. Even as friendships become more important, children still value their family and parents as sources of trustworthy information. They learn to navigate the larger world and take their place in the world through school, sports, activities, and friendships. Peer relationships gradually take a primary place. They begin to talk about the future and wonder about what it would be like to be a teen.[185]

Older elementary children will begin to notice how their bodies are changing or how other children are growing and changing. Talk about puberty with your eight- to eleven-year-old. Let them know that puberty is God's way of helping them move from a child to an adult; if we did not have puberty we would stay children forever. Even though the changes will happen over several years, it might be overwhelming for pre-teens to think about their changing bodies.

Talk to your pre-teen about how this topic can be uncomfortable and how you want to be a part of their growing up. Although it can be difficult to talk about personal things like bodies and puberty, the effort will pay off in better communication between parent and child. Tell your pre-teen that talking about our bodies and the changes that tweens will soon experience can make us feel nervous and embarrassed. This helps your pre-teen know that any feelings of nervousness or embarrassment are normal.

Although it might be awkward or embarrassing for both pre-teens and parents to talk about sexuality, keep trying. It is worth the effort for parents and pre-teens to keep the communication lines open on this topic. You may find, over time, that you have fewer of those awkward feelings. The more you talk about things, including sexuality, the more comfortable you will be.

Physical Development

- Uneven growth
- Onset of puberty for some

- Slow height gains continue
- Growth in gross and fine motor skills
- Increase in reaction time (9–11 years old)
- Growth spurt for girls may begin (9–11 years old)

Social and Emotional Development

- Growth in ability to develop and maintain friendships
- Great interest in friends outside of the family
- Friendships are the hallmarks of this period

Cognitive Development

- Significant academic growth
- Some children move from concrete thinking to abstract thinking
- Development in executive functioning skills (organizing, planning, reviewing)
- Learning to delay gratification

Spiritual and Moral Development

- Appreciate the stories and narratives of faith
- Real appreciation for the rules and what is correct
- In the earlier years, use play and imagination to explore the symbols of faith
- Benefit from the freedom to talk about what they are thinking about and their beliefs
- May begin to challenge the positions or faith of the people around them
- May understand God in human terms
- Learning to take the perspective of others
- Adopts "Golden Rule" morality

- Move from egocentric thinking to wanting to gain the approval of authority and peers
- Sense of fairness prevails, but is not always reflected in the child's behavior

Teach Me . . .

- To discuss gender and sexuality
- Conventional names for body parts
- To ask questions
- About stereotypes
- About the dangers of alcohol and drugs
- About places that are unsafe
- About non-competitive forms of activities
- That reading, writing, and arts are fun
- How to make a plan, and stick to it
- To practice with new freedoms and responsibilities
- To check in and let my parents know where I am
- That I can use parents as "an excuse" to get out of a situation
- Teach me how to value and care for myself

Here Are Some Things to Teach Your Early Elementary-Aged Child

- Our bodies are good.
- We are created by God.
- Males and females have some body parts that are different.
- As we get older, our bodies change and grow. Teach the changes that happen to boys' and girls' bodies, as they become men and women.
- Changing bodies are a normal part of life.
- Talk about pregnancy and birth. (See the teaching script for ideas of what to say on pages 192–94.)

- Name the parts of the child's body that others need permission to touch. Review ways to say "no" and how to ask for help if the child has been scared or hurt.

Vocabulary Words

- bullying
- abuse
- kissing
- love
- marriage/committed relationship
- partner
- self-esteem
- body image
- penis, testicles
- vulva, vagina
- erection
- masturbation
- labor and delivery

Discussion Questions:

1. What experience have you had with elementary-aged children?
2. What do you find joyful about this age?
3. What do you find challenging about this age?
4. What have you been told about yourself during this time of your life?
5. What do you remember about your childhood in terms of sexuality?

CHAPTER 19

ADOLESCENCE

The age between eleven and eighteen is a period of rapid change. Puberty ushers in a broad range of transitions in physical development in which children's bodies change into adults' bodies and reach sexual maturation.[186] The changes are not confined to the physical, as the cognitive, social and emotional, and moral development deepen and grow as well. Just as adolescents seem to be growing out of their not-so-right body sizes, they begin to move beyond the limiting concrete, lateral thinking to more advanced cognitive and moral thinking.

In terms of social and emotional development, adolescents are working on developing their self-image and identities. They are exploring and experimenting with who they want to be. In the early years of this developmental period, the peer group mirrors their identity; as they move through later stages, their self-image is more stable and unique. They are pushing even farther away from the nuclear family unit as they continue to challenge the social and conventional norms around them. Their responsibilities are expanding as well, as school or work become a full-time job complete with thoughts about "what is next."

SEXUAL MATURATION IN GIRLS

The budding of the breasts and a growth spurt usually signals the onset of female puberty. Menarche, or first menstruation (from the Greek word *arche*, meaning "beginning"), typically occurs relatively late in the sequence of pubertal events—around age 12½ for North American girls, 13 for Western Europeans. But the age range is wide, from 10½ to 15½ years old. Breast and pubic hair growth are completed following menarche, and underarm hair appears.

Menarche takes place after the peak of the height spurt; nature delays sexual maturity until the girl's body is large enough for childbearing. "As an extra measure of security, for twelve to eighteen months following menarche, the menstrual cycle often occurs without the release of an ovum from the ovaries. But this temporary period of sterility does not occur in all girls, and it cannot be counted on for protection against pregnancy."[187]

The Sexual Maturation of Girls[188]		
	Average in Years	**Range in Years**
Breasts begin to "bud"	10	8–13
Height spurt begins	10	8–13
Pubic hair appears	10.5	8–14
Peak strength spurt	11.6	9.5–14
Menarche occurs	12.5	10.5–13.5
Peak weight spurt	12.7	10–14
Adult stature reached	13	10–16
Pubic hair growth completed	14.5	14–15
Breast growth completed	15	10–17

SEXUAL MATURATION IN BOYS

The first sign of puberty in boys is the enlargement of the testes (glands that manufacture sperm), accompanied by changes in the texture and color of the scrotum. Pubic hair emerges soon after, about the same time the penis begins to enlarge.[189]

The Sexual Maturation of Boys[190]		
	Average in Years	Range in Years
Testes begin to enlarge	11.5	9.5–13.5
Pubic hair appears	12	10–15
Penis begins to enlarge	12	10.5–14.5
Height spurt begins	12.5	10.5–16
Spermarche (first ejaculation) occurs	13.5	12–16
Peak height spurt	14	12.5–15.5
Peak weight spurt	14	12.5–15.5
Facial hair begins to grow	14	12.5–15.5
Voice begins to deepen	14	12.5–15.5
Penis and testes growth completed	14.5	12.5–16
Peak strength spurt	15.3	13–17
Adult stature reached	15.5	13.5–17.5
Pubic hair growth completed	15.5	14–17

EARLY ADOLESCENCE (AGES 11–14)

A mix of skills and struggles characterizes early adolescence. The eleven- to fourteen-year-old is building greater communication skills and more practice with independence, yet their moods can be irregular and they struggle with impulse control.

Parents tend to focus on topics of responsibility and safety while adolescents are seeking a sense of self and independence. Parents must remember that, as teens grow, their need to develop a sense of self is vital to growing into an interdependent and emotionally healthy adult.

Messages of God, love, and acceptance are particularly important during the early teen years. Teens vacillate between concrete and abstract thinking. Talk about the sermon or Sunday-school lesson and notice how their brain is developing as their opinions emerge.

Physical Development

- Puberty begins or continues
- Physical transition from childhood to adulthood
- Displays growth in physical maturity
- Skeletal maturation
- In a span of two to four years, gain 25 percent of their adult height and 40 percent of their adult weight
- Major organs (heart, lungs, kidneys, and liver) double in size

Social and Emotional Development

- Challenges authority and parents
- Asserts independence
- Separates from parents
- Creates self-identify
- Periods of rebellion, withdrawal, and moodiness
- Movement from family to peers as the primary support system

Cognitive Development

- Development of abstract and complex thinking
- Greater intellectualizing of arguments
- Movement to autonomy

Spiritual and Moral Development

- Spiritual struggle as teens claim faith as their own
- Thinks through and applies abstract thought to moral issues
- May be very interested in church and Bible studies, or rejects religion in its formal state
- Struggles with ethics and fairness
- Period of convention and conformity

Teach Me . . . (Older Elementary)

- The distinction between biological sex, sexual attraction, sexual identity, and sexual expression
- The connection between my faith and my sexuality, building on my understanding of my place in creation
- How to practice excellent listening skills
- To speak to trustworthy adults
- A review of basic reproductive anatomy
- The definition of sexual intercourse
- To ask questions to qualify and understand my perspective
- About values
- About puberty and share information about changes that will occur as my body changes
- Specific strategies to deal with the changes of puberty: who to ask for information, how to ask for help, where to find pads/tampons, advice on shaving, basic hygiene, and so on
- Affirm my community: God gave us friends and family to love and support one another
- About pregnancy and birth

Reach Out to Teach Me (or Let Me Teach You) . . . (Middle School Age)

- Seek to see Christ in me
- Remind me of my gifts

Common Sense Media is a website that helps parents, teachers, and other adults by providing information and tools for the use of media and technology in the life of kids. www.commonsensemedia.org/

- Continue to find ways to play physically with me—scratching my back, playing a contact game, or wrestling will keep you close to me
- Move from my director to my coach
- Accept some criticism aimed at you—I must push against you to learn who I want to be
- Balance your parental concerns with my needs to grow in independence
- Use teachable moments to connect faith with my everyday life
- Use door openers to learn more about what I am thinking and feeling
- Review anatomy and physiology
- Discuss health in terms of body, soul, and mind
- Discuss sexually transmitted infections (STIs)
- Introduce the concept of safer sex
- Answer my emotionally charged questions with a spirit of honesty and non-judgment
- Teach me decision-making processes
- Develop a password that I can use when I need to leave an unsafe situation
- Talk about the media, TV, the Internet, and the role that they each play in our lives

Vocabulary Words

- wet dreams
- ejaculation
- pubic hair
- puberty

- parts of female anatomy: fallopian tubes, ovaries, uterus, cervix, vagina, vulva, clitoris, clitoral hood, labia, urethral opening, perineum, breasts, areola, nipple, mammary glands
- parts of male anatomy: shaft, scrotum, perineum, prostrate, urethra, vas deferens, testicle, glans, foreskin
- self-breast exam
- self-testicular exam
- dating
- intercourse
- sex
- birth control
- condoms
- gender identity
- sexual orientation
- LGBTQ+

MIDDLE ADOLESCENCE (AGES 15–18)

By middle adolescence, teens are gaining a better sense of self and identity. Relationships are fluid as friendships evolve and change quickly. Teens fifteen to eighteen years old move farther away from parents emotionally, placing a greater emphasis on peer groups, competition, and competence. Even as their confidence grows, their self-doubt creeps back into the forefront of their emotional lives. Their mood swings may exhibit feelings of sadness as their secured place in the family unit begins to change. Listen for your teen's self-talk and help reshape the messages they are sending themselves to positive affirming messages.

Parents can create more intentional family time that invites the teen to enter in on their own terms. Giving more control over choices and responsibilities to the teen will help with their needs for independence.

As teens begin to contemplate life after high school, they may begin to develop a greater sense of identity. Talk about when they have experienced their best selves. When did they feel God smiling at them?

Physical Development

- Preoccupation with self-image
- Most are nearly through or have completed puberty
- Growth spurts for boys may continue
- Reduction in variation of sexual development; sexual development is varied in earlier years (everyone is *not* at the same stage of sexual development)
- Beginning to be more comfortable in their bodies, as the rapid changes ebb

Social and Emotional Development

- Growth in autonomy
- May build stronger relationships and bonds
- Interest in romantic relationships
- May prepare for leaving home
- Increased control of feelings, less impulsive
- Appreciative of family and support systems
- Intense experimentation around identity, relationships, possible careers, and sexuality

Cognitive Development

- Tends to argue rather than discuss
- Learning to apply if/then thinking to new situations
- Measures others' actions in relation to a "fairness rule"[191]
- Becoming more comfortable with gray areas, but still tends to think in dualistic terms
- Increasingly able to experience adults as real, flawed people, rather than idealized role-models

- Develops a sense of personal awareness and the ability to reflect
- Benefits from conversation with adult when their thoughts, feelings, and positions are valued
- Uneven cognitive and social development (may argue for a position and then do the opposite)

Spiritual and Moral Development

- Seeks social approval as a basis of decision-making
- Wants to think well of themselves (preserve self-esteem)
- Rationalizes actions
- Begins to experience conflict between the dominate culture and familial culture
- Understands the concept of a dilemma
- May reject family value system in order to solidify a personal moral code
- Searching for what they can "believe in"
- Evidence of a developing code of personal behavior
- May be more generous in relationships
- Greater ability to see a variety of perspectives yields increased empathy
- Begins to see the bigger picture
- Begins to value personal moral virtues over "laws"

Teach Me . . .

- That you are supportive of my need for independence
- How to build a code of life for myself
- Ways to evaluate options and weigh choices
- By modeling self-control, faith, delaying gratification, and impulse control
- That discussing ideas and concepts is important and interesting
- That you accept me by listening to me and valuing my opinion

- How to handle difficult decisions, by sharing your struggles and dilemmas
- How I handle a mistake can change a mistake into positive life changing experience
- What is important to you, by asking what's important to me
- The basics of self-care
- How to live on my own

Conversation Starters

- Recognize God as a part of all of our relationships, including our most intimate relationships.
- Think about our friendships, romantic relationships, and our bodies in light of Jesus's commandment: "Love each other. Just as I have loved you, so you must love each other" (John 13:34).
- Talk about ethics and morality in the news.
- Talk about dating, including how to break up in a kind and gentle way.
- Practice models of decision-making.
- Move from coach to advisor.
- Model effective self-talk and messages.
- Review personal care and health areas.
- Talk about moral dilemmas.
- Ask about what they value and how they are feeling.
- Talk about their gifts and help identify strengths that you see.
- Use current events to launch conversations.
- Model relationship skills like listening, empathy, effective confrontation, and problem-solving.

As with each previous age, **reviewing key vocabulary words** is important as some definitions may evolve as children grow into teenagers and then into adulthood.

- Talk about the role of friendships in your life.
- Make sure your teen knows when they are sick and what to do if they are.

Vocabulary Words

- parts of female anatomy: fallopian tubes, ovaries, uterus, cervix, vagina, vulva, clitoris, clitoral hood, labia, urethral opening, perineum, breasts, areola, nipple, mammary glands
- parts of male anatomy: shaft, scrotum, perineum, prostrate, urethra, vas deferens, testicle, glans, foreskin
- self-breast exam
- self-testicular exam
- dating
- dating violence
- date rape
- sexual assault
- intercourse
- sex
- birth control
- condoms
- significant other/partner
- assertiveness

LATE ADOLESCENCE (AGES 17–19)

Late adolescents express themselves clearly and thoughtfully. They exhibit greater emotional stability, yet their problem-solving and decision-making skills are still not fully developed. They are moving toward a firmer identity and can stand their ground against social pressure more easily. Greater concern for others translates into deeper and more meaningful relationships. They have the capacity for more intimate relationships characterized by tenderness and love.

Their movement to adulthood is almost complete and they may be able to self-regulate their emotional state and self-esteem.

Late adolescents benefit from trusted people who can be a sounding board for their ideas, interests, and problems. As they navigate the world on their own terms, friendships deepen and their ability to discern choices for themselves becomes apparent. The mix of adult behaviors and adolescent struggles that linger often surprises parents.

Conversation Starters

- Move from advisor to trusted listener.
- Talk about your faith and the connection between your faith and your everyday life.
- Ask questions that help clarify the issue at hand.
- Be sensitive to more complex emotional states.
- Affirm their decision-making processes and choices.
- Remind them of their gifts.

Vocabulary Words and Concepts

- responsibility
- adulthood
- discernment
- spiritual growth
- gifts
- communication styles
- self-awareness
- relationship skills
- negotiation
- assertiveness
- self-help skills
- goal setting
- resilience

- healthy habits
- self-disciple
- self-esteem and confidence
- risk assessment
- life-management skills

Discussion Questions:

1. What experience have you had with teenagers?
2. What do you find joyful about this age?
3. What do you find challenging about this age?
4. What have you been told about yourself during this time of your life?
5. What do you remember about your teen years in terms of your sexuality: milestones of puberty, social experiences, and first sexual experiences?

PART IV

THE
PRACTICAL

Most parents want to teach values to their children and be the main source of information about sex and ethical responsibility, but they often need help in this process of moral formation. The bishop is right that congregations are ideal places to offer value-based sexuality education and that faith-based programs can easily complement what parents do at home. To be worthwhile, a sexual ethic must attend to be the pleasures as well as the dangers of sexuality in this culture and manage to keep both in perspective. When a young person or anyone else is made ignorant about sexuality, they are placed at greater risk of being harmed and possibly of doing harm.

—Marvin Ellison[192]

CHAPTER 20

THE NEED FOR CONVERSATION

There are too few sexuality education programs that empower parents to have knowledgeable conversations with their children. Children need more information to build the confidence that will allow them to make healthier choices. It is the lack of information that has real and negative consequences on our youth.

There is a great need for open, caring conversation; so many statistics show what happens when those conversations don't happen. For example, "Sixty percent of sexually active teens admit to regretting their first time, which can lead to low self-esteem, shame, and depression."[193] Furthermore, according to the Center for Disease Control's Division of STD Prevention, "Prevalence estimates suggest that young people aged 15–24 years acquire half of all new sexually transmitted infections (STI). Compared with older adults, sexually active adolescents aged 15–19 years and young adults aged 20–24 years are at higher risk of acquiring STDs for a combination of behavioral, biological, and cultural reasons."[194]

How we understand our bodies and sexuality significantly affects our spiritual lives. Research shows that young people report having fewer conversations about sex and sexual values than their parents claim to have. A nation-wide survey shows that while a majority of parents say they talk with youth about healthy relationships, very few are tackling birth control.[195] The research shows "that youth were much less likely to have initiated sexual intercourse if their parents taught them to say no, set clear rules, talked about what is right and wrong, and about delaying sexual activity. If youth were sexually active, they were more likely to use birth control if taught at home about delaying sexual activity and about birth control."[196]

Youth are much more likely to make safe, healthy choices about their bodies the more frequently their parents talk with them about their bodies, how to delay sex, how to say no, using birth control, and healthy relationships. It is vital that parents begin conversations early and frequently in children's lives.[197] All of this research compels us to tackle these topics in intentional, direct, and empowering ways.

AIMS—TALK

The Aims of Education[198] by Nel Noddings addresses the purpose of aims-talk in the educational system. Aims-talk focuses on the deepest questions in education: What are we doing and *why* are we doing it? As the times change, our aims must take on newer, richer meanings.

Currently our school systems are driven by standards of learning that determine what every student should learn; many claim that this forces teachers to teach to the test. As a society, we do not ask if the education our children are receiving is appropriate. Are there clear aims for sexuality education in public schools? Do the aims meet the needs of society? Does the Church have an aim for education? Does the Church have an aim for sexuality education? What is that aim? An aim of the Church should be engaging the whole self, including our sexuality. "As sensuous human beings, we know and value the world and therefore become self-directing moral agents only as we feel connected in and through our bodies . . . 'all our relations to others—

to God, to neighbor, to cosmos—[are] mediated through our bodies, which are the locus of our perception and knowledge of the world.'"[199]

Schools and parents also struggle with how to respond to individuals who struggle with gender identity or who clearly identify with another gender. Daniel Heischman, Executive Director of the National Association of Episcopal Schools writes, "In the independent and private school world, the question of how best to respond to people who begin to identify with another gender has become significant; in fact, we are confident these questions will impact all of our schools, including posing unique challenges for single sex schools."[200] It is important to recognize that the question of how best to respond goes beyond educating students. Teachers and parents need education as well. And it is not isolated to schools; parishes and summer camp settings also must address the question of how best to respond.

We must identify our own prejudices and our fears when figuring out how to respond to our LGBTQ+ members. We are called and challenged to get to know individuals, to listen to their stories. We are all more than the labels put upon us or that we take on.

THE PRONOUNS WE USE

One of the ways we can be welcoming to people is to ask them how they want to be addressed. Just like calling someone by the correct name or using ma'am or sir when some prefers it, using the correct pronouns a person prefers is very important to honoring their identity and personhood. Just like our gender expression and gender identity, pronouns are non-binary; they are not limited to opposing opposites, but allow fluid expression across a spectrum. English does not have a "gender neutral or third gender pronoun available, and this has been criticized, since in many instances, writers, speakers, etc. use 'he/his' when referring to a generic individual in the third person. Also, the dichotomy of 'he and she' in English does not leave room for other gender identities, which is a source of frustration to the transgender and genderqueer communities."[201]

"A gender neutral or gender inclusive pronoun is a pronoun which does not associate a gender with the individual who is being discussed."[202] There are a variety of pronouns people choose to use for themselves: She/Her/Hers/Herself, He/Him/His/Himself, They/Them/Theirs/Themself, Ze/Hir/Zir/Hirs/Zirs/Hirself/Zirself. Both the University of Wisconsin at Milwaukee's Lesbian, Gay, Bisexual, Transgender Resource Center and Trans Student Educational Resources (TSER) offer excellent gender pronouns graphics and history to help us understand their use. Below is a chart explaining the use of pronouns, adapted from TSER. Please note that these are not the only pronouns. There are an infinite number of pronouns as new ones emerge in our language. Always ask someone for their pronouns.

Gender Pronouns				
Subjective	Objective	Possessive	Reflexive	Example
She	Her	Hers	Herself	She is speaking. I listened to her. The backpack is hers.
He	Him	His	Himself	He is speaking. I listened to him. The backpack is his.
They	Them	Theirs	Themself	They are speaking. I listened to them. The backpack is theirs.
Ze	Hir/Zir	Hirs/Zirs	Hirself/Zirself	Ze is speaking. I listened to hir. The backpack is zirs.

When we are thinking about how to welcome LGBTQ+ brothers and sisters, the command to love one another and our neighbors should be our guiding value. We know that the most loving thing to do is to provide an environment that is not only safe, but welcoming. Advanced planning involving bathrooms, changing areas, sleeping areas and group norms should be part of the first steps. This can be challenging to a system that traditionally works in a prescribed way. "We have always done it this way" is a common first blush response. Our systems that do not actively seek to include LGBTQ+ prohibit them from participating.

BATHROOMS AND BEDROOMS

When seeking to meet the needs of transgender and non-conforming children and teens, youth leaders need to ask the preference of LGBTQ+ persons. Their perspective of what would make them most comfortable might be difficult to express on their own. Youth leaders can empower youth to tell the leaders what would help them to feel comfortable and safe.

Some people may feel most comfortable when a separate sleeping area or non-gender specific bathrooms are available. LGBTQ+ persons should be provided a neutral, private bathroom in which to change and shower. Many transgender or non-conforming youth are not comfortable using gender-segregated bathrooms. LGBTQ+ youth should also be given a place to sleep where they are comfortable. This may be that they sleep alongside the gender with which they most identify. Some leaders have expressed concern that this could worry parents of other children in the program, or make other children uncomfortable. Remember that our LGBTQ+ children are in the minority and their needs and concerns are paramount. The same is true when working with LGBTQ+ adults.

The Gay, Lesbian & Straight Education Network explains how to make all individuals feel safe and welcome:

In any gender-segregated facility, any student who is uncomfortable using a shared facility, regardless of the reason, shall, upon the student's request, be provided with a safe and non-stigmatizing alternative. This may include, for example, addition of a privacy partition or curtain, provision to use a nearby private restroom or office, or a separate changing schedule. However, requiring a transgender or gender non-conforming student to use a separate, nonintegrated space threatens to publicly identify and marginalize the student as transgender and should not be done unless requested by a student. Under no circumstances may students be required to use sex-segregated facilities that are inconsistent with their gender identity.[203]

COMING OUT

Lesbian, gay, bisexual, and transgender people have better self-esteem and less depression as young adults if they were open about their sexual orientation as adolescents.[204] Many young people disclose at school, and many will disclose in church, especially as the faith community becomes more hospitable and safe. Those adults who minister with middle school or high school youth can expect that at some point in their ministry a young person will "come out" to them and/or the youth group.

Daniel Heischman reminds his constituency (NAES) about the need to be prepared, aware, and open. His remarks can also be applied to our churches:

Ultimately, issues such as these quickly go from being abstract matters to real human stories. . . . As we enter into this new landscape for our culture and our schools, we are confident that individuals and communities will encounter many blessings, not the least being an enhanced understanding of what it means to be human and to be a part of a community of grace and reconciliation.[205]

Below are some suggestions that meet the standard of both love and safety offered by PFLAG that can help parents and adult leaders.

Tips for Professionals Who Work with LGBT Youth

1. **Don't be surprised when a youth "comes out" to you.** They have tested you with a series of "trial balloons" over a period of time. Based on your previous responses they've decided you can be trusted and helpful.

2. **Respect confidentiality.** If a lesbian, gay, bisexual, transgender (LGBT) or questioning youth shares with you information about their sexual orientation or gender identity, you have a trust that must be respected. A breach of this confidence has led some to suicide.

3. **Be informed and examine your own biases.** Most of us are the products of a homophobic and transphobic society influenced by misinformation and fear. You can't be free of it just by deciding to; read reliable sources and talk to qualified persons.

4. **Know when and where to seek help.** Know the referral agencies and counselors in your area. LGBT helplines can provide you with professional persons and organizations that are qualified to help. Tell them who you are and what kind of assistance you need. They'll be helpful and fair. You can reach PFLAG NYC at 212-463-0629.

5. **Maintain a balanced perspective.** Sexual thoughts and feelings are only a small (but important) part of a person's personality.

6. **Understand the meaning of sexual orientation and gender identity.** Each person's sexual orientation and gender identity is what is natural to that person. It is not a matter of sexual "preference." People do not choose to be gay, lesbian,

bisexual, or transgender; they simply are. One's sense of gender identity is a separate issue with unique complexities and challenges.

7. **Deal with feelings first.** Most LGBT youth feel alone, afraid, and guilty. You can assist by listening, thus allowing them to release feelings and thoughts that are often in conflict.

8. **Be supportive. Explain that many people have struggled with these issues in the past.** Admit that dealing with one's sexuality or a gender identity that is different from one's birth sex is difficult. There are no easy and fast answers, whether heterosexual, bisexual, gay, lesbian, or transgender. Keep the door open for more conversations and assistance. Be aware that so-called "reparative therapy" has been discredited by all major mental health professional associations and can be harmful. While some groups promote it, it is not a credible way of offering support.

9. **Anticipate some confusion.** Most youth are sure of their sexual orientation by the time they finish the eighth grade and the same appears to be true with gender identity. But some young people will be confused and unsure. They have to work through their own feeling and insights; you can't talk them into, or out of, being gay, lesbian, bisexual, or transgender.

10. **Help, but do not force.** If you are heterosexual or comfortable with your birth sex, you probably do not understand what it means to be different in these ways. Clues for how you can help will come from the young person. Don't force them into your frame of reference to make it easier for you to understand.

11. **Don't try to guess who is LGBT.** It is not helpful for you or for the youth you serve. We live in a world of stereotypes

that do people an injustice; do not be tempted to perpetuate old myths.

12. **Challenge homophobic remarks and jokes.** Speak up when someone makes disparaging remarks about LGBTQ people, or thoughtlessly uses anti-gay language, just as you would any other slurs. Don't perpetuate injustice through silence.[206]

Faith communities can partner with parents in ensuring our children and youth receive information about their bodies and sexuality in a safe environment. Church members can serve as role models and mentors to younger members as part of a holistic, lifelong faith formation program. "As a Church that has always stood for justice and dignity we are compelled to include gender expression and gender identity in our statement of who we are and who is the *all* when we talk about *all* people in Christ."[207]

Discussion Questions:

1. Did you ever have "the talk" with your parent? How do you remember this? What would you have wanted to be different, if anything?
2. Who (or what) was your main source of information regarding sex?
3. What kinds of conversations have you had in your faith community about sexuality?
4. What kinds of conversations would you like to have in your faith community about sexuality?
5. Has your family, congregation, or youth group discussed how to be accepting of an individual who may "come out" in the community?

CHAPTER 21

PARENTS ARE THE KEY

The most effective teaching about sexuality includes both children and parents. If you are a parent, you know that your children have been watching you and learning from you since birth. Your most basic gestures, attitudes, and comments teach your children how to think about their bodies. You already teach them about bathing, toilet training, dressing, safety, and nutrition. Teaching conversations with your child continue into their pre-teen years. Your teaching will change to include routine hygiene, sleep habits, loving friendships, changing bodies, and handling puberty. Parents sometimes feel anxious about tackling the next stage of questions and we want to give you the information you need so you can jump right into conversations with your child or teen, instead of shying away from these "touchy" topics.

Although you are not the only source of information for your child, you are the primary educator—you are the most consistent, the most present, and the most responsive. You are the one who can give them a foundation of values, attitudes, and skills that will guide them into their young adult years. The realization that you are the primary sexuality educator of your child can be the beginning of an exciting journey, and the entryway to a host of parental anxieties and questions.

Many parents feel unprepared for this phase of parenting. When your child enters puberty, your voice needs to be heard—your voice on sex, your voice on behavior, your voice on attitudes, and your voice on how faith connects to sexuality. How do you make that happen?

Even the basic anatomy and physiology can be a barrier to open communication about puberty. Many parents realize that they need to be a part of the conversations about sexuality with their children, but sense a divide between their family's values and the values their children receive from advertisements and entertainment. It sometimes feels like these industries are hijacking our families. We hear parents ask for guidance in crafting messages to their teens; they want messages that combat selfish and cynical messages about love, bodies, and sex. Parents want truthful messages that challenge the incomplete and stunted teachings our children receive from our modern culture. They want messages that connect faith and sexuality and messages that ask, "Where is God in this?"

SEXUALITY EDUCATION EXPERIENCES

In many schools, children and teens take health education or human sexuality classes; however, those classes usually focus only on physiology and reproductive organs and sometimes are offered too late in a child's development. Acknowledging that the quality of these programs varies by school, many lack a rigorous parental component. Unfortunately, school programs are not able to help parents answer the questions they will most likely be asked at home. School programs cannot help students connect their faith and values.

Parents do not always have positive memories of their own sexuality education. When we ask adults how they learned about sex and what they would change, we get a myriad of answers. Some found a book on their bed without any explanation; others had no conversations or education from their parents at all. Some people received incorrect anxiety-producing and unhelpful advice from older siblings.

We also hear stories, however, of families growing together. Some adults tell of a dynamic relationship with a parent who talked with them and not at them, or a parent who approached sexuality and sex with humor or an attitude of celebration, rather than judgment. Those parents often provided a healthy model for sexuality education as an ongoing process.

A WAY FORWARD

Today, we have many resources to help children and adults of all ages learn about their bodies and sexuality. There is much for all of us to learn when it comes to sexuality, our bodies, and our faith. Grab a resource, grab a friend, and have a conversation—parents do not have to go it alone. Here is a guide to help start thinking about what children need to learn:

- They need accurate information and knowledge that they will not have to re-learn.
- They need skills that they can use as they grow and experience new things.
- They need values to navigate a world they have never experienced—values which will anchor them in their faith, giving them a way to safely grow and learn.

Through the *These Are Our Bodies* program modules, children, youth, and parents are provided words, the confidence, and the road map to navigate the next few years. The following chapters provide a guide for all those working with kids of any age on what to expect developmentally, how to ask and answer questions, and suggestions for making faith connections. For more information to help you along this journey, look to the *These Are Our Bodies* age-level program modules and the suggested resources found at the conclusion of this book.

Discussion Questions:

1. If you are a parent, what have you spoken to your children about in terms of sex and their sexuality? What worked/didn't work? Where could you use some help?

2. If you are a church leader, have you offered classes or conversation with parents about human sexuality? What worked, what didn't work?

3. What types of sexuality education is offered in your local school system? At what age/s? What is the content?

CHAPTER 22

TEACHABLE MOMENTS

Sexuality education is a process. We know that the best way to develop a relationship with our children is over time, and with patience, generosity, and good humor. Most effective teaching and guiding are done at a glacial pace. Basic instruction and plenty of reinforcement over weeks or months are the stalwarts of parenting. Jenny (one of the authors) remembers teaching her children to tie their shoes. She and her husband talked about tying shoes, they modeled how to tie shoes, they shared with their children why it was important to learn, and they encouraged them. Most of all, they practiced and retaught. It was not a one-time talk or even a one-time demonstration—it was a process.

We know that the one-time sex talk is insufficient to build a strong foundation of values, skills, and information. Most parents and teens remember "the talk" as a stressful and painful experience; it is time we let that model go! A set of give-and-take short conversations over many years works best. Parents who acknowledge the change

> The **one-time sex talk** is insufficient to build a strong foundation of values, skills, and information.

and growth of their children's bodies in positive ways help provide a sense of goodness about the body.

These small teachable moments in your life together—as parent and child—are the framework for inviting conversation, giving timely information, and building trust. Most parents tell us that they want to be the person their children and teens come to when they have questions; they want to be present and engaged for their children. Parents want their children to have the information and knowledge they need. Parents want to impart values and wisdom that will help them live a faithful life. Teens want to know that their parents understand what they are experiencing.

SEXUALITY AS A GIFT FROM GOD

As people of faith we know that whenever we talk about sexuality, there is a story to be shared: We are all God's precious children and our sexuality is a gift. Our sexuality is a gift from God and considered to be an essential part of our humanness. Connecting our sexuality to our lives and the lives of our children is a natural part of our living faith.[208]

Kelly Brown Douglas, the author of *What's Faith Got to Do With It? Black Bodies/Christian Souls* (Maryknoll, NY: Orbis Books, 2005), argues that "sexuality is inexplicably linked to Christianity, and that the positive evaluation of sexuality is essential to one's relationship . . . with God." We are made in the image of God and our very creation is affirmed as good—and that includes our sexuality. "Sexuality, and all of its mystery, is about who we are as relational beings," she said. "A person's ability to enter into right relationship with God corresponds to one's ability to affirm who he or she is as a sexual being."[209]

MAKING A FAITH CONNECTION

Christian parents wonder: How do I communicate that faith connection to my child? How can I provide an environment where my children can ask the questions they need to ask? How can I answer their questions in a way that helps them to experience faith as a source of strength, encouragement, and joy?

Making the faith connection can be one of the most difficult parts of talking to our children and teens about sexuality and bodies. The confusion around sexuality and faith in our society very often encourages us not to speak about our beliefs. How do we express our deepest beliefs in a way that will help our young people grow into the adults that God has designed them to be?

Find teachable moments to talk about *your* values with your child or teen. If you are fortunate enough to have Christian friends who will engage in conversation, talk to them about your conversations and ask them to share how they communicate with their children. Helping our children grow into the "fullness of Christ" (Ephesians 4:13) is the perfect example of Christian community—community that supports, loves, encourages, and informs. Your child will benefit from knowing how your values inform your choices, beliefs, and actions. As your teen grows in faith, those faith connections will help them see the world through the eyes of a child of God. And for that we are grateful.

Remember when it comes to talking about difficult subjects like sexuality, it is not a five-minute "talk"—it is about building an ongoing conversation, a dialogue that focuses on the questions, not the answers. As your children grow up, they need more knowledge and information. Starting early with an eye to teachable moments will propel your relationship and your ability to talk honestly with your child.

The better you communicate, the more at ease you will feel about discussing sex, relationships, and faith.

Listen Carefully

Listen for what your child is not saying. Are they confused? nervous? scared? Address their need to understand their own emotions as well as their need for knowledge.

Be Honest

Admit when you do not know an answer and tell your child that you will find out the answer. Let your child know that you are learning too and you need some practice talking about these personal topics. Vulnerability and empathy build connection with others.

Teach Values

Values give children the foundation to make decisions on their own. Values will guide them when parents or trusted adults are not there to give advice or directions. Give your child the facts and attach your values to every conversation.

Use the Media

TV reports, commercials, radio, and movies can be used as teachable moments to help you introduce a subject in a natural, unforced way. The goal is to make conservations about sexuality commonplace and

For more on **vulnerability and empathy**, see Dr. Brené Brown's work, especially *Gifts of Imperfection: Let Go of Who You Think You're Supposed to Be and Embrace Who You Are, The Daring Way: How the Courage to be Vulnerable Transforms the Way We Live, Love, Parent, and Lead, and Rising Strong.* http://brenebrown.com/

frequent in your home. The more you talk about sexuality, the easier the conversations will become. Turn up the radio and talk about the lyrics. Watch the more mature movie and talk about what your child or teen saw.

Use Door Openers

A door opener is a statement that keeps the door of the conversation open. It invites conversations and shows interest. Try, "Tell me more about that," "I am interested in hearing what you think," or "Tell me how that makes you feel." Using door openers will allow you to teach your child how to reflect their behavior, choices, and the world around them.

Keep Your Child Safe

Role-play with your child and practice ways of getting out of difficult situations. Teach your child a code phrase that they can use when they need to get home fast. For example, they could call home and say they have a stomachache; the parent would immediately know that they wanted to come home due to something they cannot say out loud.

Discussion Questions:

1. Recall a "teachable moment" in your own life having to do with sexuality that either was addressed or missed the mark.
2. Recall a "teachable moment" in your relationship with a child or teen that was either addressed or missed. What would you have done differently?
3. How can you better connect faith with sexuality, for yourself and those you care for, either at church or home?

CHAPTER 23

GETTING STARTED

When is the right time to talk to children and teens about sexuality, bodies, and faith? Some might say that it is best to wait until the child brings up the subject—that is one approach. On the other hand, many sexuality educators will tell you that it is best to teach people about changes before they happen. For adolescents, that means teaching them about eighteen months before puberty begins. Puberty is made up of predictable milestones, yet brings a set of challenges and surprises for both teens and parents. Everyone goes through puberty in a similar pattern; however, it is hard to know the exact time that puberty will start. It is never too late to start conversations about changing bodies, changing relationships, and the connection between faith and sexuality.

By late elementary to middle school, children are recognizing that their friends are changing and growing. Teens naturally have questions about those changes and their own changing bodies. Sometimes their search for answers bypasses parents altogether, as they gain information about puberty from friends, neighbors, and siblings. Parents may not realize how much their teens have already been told by others. Although pre-teens and early teens may seem too young—still innocent children—they are usually already much further into the world of puberty than parents might realize. Teens are mostly concerned about getting the facts straight. Their primary concern is: What happens when? When is it going to happen to me? Teens want order in their world along with an idea of what is coming next. And Christian parents want to be a part of that dynamic conversation.

Another reason to engage in conversation in this window is a developmental one—it is the right time in a child's life. Teens are developmentally open to hearing information. They can have insightful conversations with adults about new topics at school, headlines in the paper, or what they learned in Sunday school. They have mastered the basics of school and are good at processing and applying information. The same can be expected of conversations about sexuality.

Teens are receptive to hearing information from their parents. For the most part, they still see parents as trustworthy sources of guidance in times of confusion and conflict. As teens mature, some will turn more toward their peer group as the first source of information.

VESSELS WAITING TO BE FILLED

Let's imagine that your child is a vase, a receptacle for information and values. The parent is a pitcher, constantly providing a steady stream of information and values to their young vessel. When children are young the mouth of the vase is wide and accepting of the information that their parents give them. Parents of young children are in no hurry, occasionally dribbling in little drips—a fact here, a value there—into the vase. Parents are filling the vase with raindrops, at times forgetting to attach values or skills to instructions. Parents give their children droplets of content and context throughout their lives (whether intentional or not), and perhaps postponing the most crucial information.

As children get older and grow into tweens and teens, two things happen: The mouth of the vase begins to close and the parent's pitcher seems to triple in size. Adolescents are naturally less receptive to their parents' guidance and advice. Older teens begin to doubt our answers; they push us away and look outside the family for the answers to their immediate questions.

Parents change as well. Parents sense their teens' withdrawal and their hesitation to tell us about their lives. At the same time, parents recognize this unstable, demanding, and often unforgiving world in which our teenagers must learn to live. Seemingly overnight, parents have an urgent desire to impart all of our knowledge and values. The parental pitcher becomes overloaded. Parents begin to pour values at a fire-hose strength into a vase whose mouth is closing. They panic: What's most important to communicate?

This analogy illustrates that *now* is the time to communicate, to share our values, and to teach decision-making strategies. *Now* is the time that your children are most receptive to explicit messages from you about life-giving wisdom, facts, and values. The challenge begins with learning to pour a stronger, steadier stream of messages during this time of receptivity. The strong, steady pour is the best way of imparting your values. As parents we sometimes hesitate to discuss our beliefs; perhaps we are embarrassed or fear that people will perceive us as overbearing. Meanwhile, our society, schools, and neighborhoods are imparting their own steady stream of values— and they are not embarrassed nor are they hesitating. Your call as a parent is to pick up your pitcher and start pouring now.

BEGIN EARLY

What about waiting until they ask? Parents sometimes wait until their teens are interested enough to ask them questions. Some children do begin asking questions, even in preschool; parents of these children are fortunate to have a simple entry into conversations. Other parents will have to create teachable moments in their children's lives in order to impart the information and values that their children need to hear. Many of the things parents teach children are taught before the child exhibits a need or an interest in learning. For example, parents do not wait to teach young children about manners. Most parents begin teaching manners as soon as babies begin to interact with others. They certainly do not wait until Henry asks, "What is this napkin for?" or "How do I use a spoon?" Using the same reasoning, why wait to talk about one of the most important parts of your child's life? Why avoid conversations when you can be imparting values to your child?

It is tempting to postpone these conversations because talking about sexuality seems so much harder than talking about manners. It doesn't have to be . . . we promise.

Discussion Questions:

1. When did you begin conversations with your children about sexuality?
2. What plan can you establish to make this an ongoing conversation in the future?
3. To whom can you turn for support?

CHAPTER 24

WHEN TO BEGIN THE CONVERSATION

If a parent wants to be the person to tell their child about sexual intercourse and its place in God's creation, parents will need to beat their peers and neighbors to the punch. We have all heard of families in which Santa was unveiled prematurely and parents wished they could turn back time. In the real world we can sometimes protect our children from hearing the truth about Santa or the tooth fairy, but it is very difficult to keep our children from hearing about sex from people outside the home. Children often hear about sex and babies from a neighbor, cousin, or the person sitting next to them on the bus. Teaching our children about sexuality and laying that faith foundation is much too important to postpone.

Begin the conversation in infancy. We are teaching our kids about their sexuality when we teach them about their body. When we teach them the names of their anatomy: fingers, toes, penis, vagina, . . . The names of your body parts are simply that, the name the parts are called. The value in them is not the name, it is in how we use them or do not use them. How can your child tell you their stomach hurts if you never teach them what their stomach is? This is true for all of our body parts.

If you want to be the first voice on the subject, tell your child how babies "get in and out" before kindergarten. Below is a suggested script used in families like yours with a five-year-old. The story is in three parts with a "refrain" of value statements that can be repeated after each telling. It is best to tell the story in three short parts with several weeks in between. If you are pregnant or know someone who is pregnant, use that as fodder for your teachable moments. Take our advice: It is much easier to tell a five-year-old how a baby is born than it is to tell an eleven-year-old. You can use pets as a teaching tool as well. "Spot is going to the vet so that he cannot have babies. The doctor cuts the tube that carries sperm, so that he will not have any more sperm. Without sperm, Spot cannot have puppies with a female dog."

TIPS

- Remember to approach the topic in a matter-of-fact way.
- Use simple language and clear concepts that will not have to be unlearned. One family taught their child that babies grow in the stomach. When the child learned about the digestive system, she was *very* confused. Aim to tell your children the truth as best as you can.
- Use correct terminology. When parents use the correct terminology, concepts do not have to be unlearned or re-taught. You want your children to have the basics on which they can build their understanding as they grow.

A SCRIPT FOR A YOUNG CHILD

Parent: God made a special way for babies to be made. You know that it takes an egg and a sperm to make a baby. The male gives the sperm and the female gives the egg. The egg and the sperm come together and grow inside the female's pelvis in a special place called the uterus. The uterus is like a nest for babies. It gives the baby a safe place to grow and good nutrition for the forty weeks that it needs to grow and develop. Do you have any questions about that part?

Refrain: Remember that God created this plan. It might seem complicated or confusing. When you have questions, come to me. I will answer all your questions. You might even hear things at school or on the playground; know that we can talk about those things as well. I love YOU!

(A Few Weeks Later)

Parent: What you might not know is exactly how the egg and the sperm get together. There are several ways that an egg and sperm can get together. One way is for a male and female to have sexual intercourse. You know that a male has a penis. A female has a vagina. The male puts his penis inside the female's vagina. The sperm comes out of the top of the penis. The sperm are propelled through the uterus into the fallopian tube where the sperm meet the egg. Once the egg and the sperm come together, it is now called a fertilized egg or embryo. Do you have any questions about that part?

Refrain

(A Few Weeks Later)

Parent: The fertilized egg lives in a special sack called the uterus. You have seen someone who is pregnant, right? Remember that the baby is growing inside the woman's uterus—that is the real name for the sack that protects the baby and helps it to grow. When the baby is ready to be born, the woman's body helps push the baby out through the woman's vagina. Women and girls have three holes: the anus, where bowel movements come out, the vagina where the baby comes out, and the urinary opening, where urine or pee-pee comes out. God made the vagina so that it can stretch and become the birth canal for the baby. The baby comes out between the female's legs. The way that babies are created and the way that they are born is a miracle of God's creation. Do you have any questions about that part?

Refrain

MORE CONVERSATION STARTERS FOR AN OLDER CHILD

Parent: Sometimes couples have a hard time conceiving (conceiving is another way of describing the egg and sperm coming together inside the female). Fortunately, doctors can help some couples have babies. One way a doctor can help is by taking the sperm from a male and putting it into the female's vagina or uterus. Another way a doctor can help is by taking eggs from a female and sperm from a male; then the doctor can put the sperm and the eggs together outside of the female's body. Once the egg or eggs are fertilized, the embryos are implanted into the female's uterus to grow.

Parent: Remember that there are many ways to make a family. Some families have two moms, others have two dads, and some have a mom or a dad. Some couples decide to adopt children. Not all families look alike. The most important thing about a family is that they love each other.

Parent: Sometimes a woman becomes pregnant and finds that she is unable to care for a baby. Sometimes a couple makes this decision. Sometimes teenagers or young people decide that they cannot raise their babies. Some people decide to place their baby for adoption, so another family that wants to have a baby to love can care for the baby. Even though it is sad for a mother or a couple to ask someone else to raise their baby, adoption can be the answer to another family's prayers.

A NOTE ABOUT ADOPTION

God can transform our sad and painful experiences in unexpected ways. When we talk about adoption, we use the word "place" for a good reason. In the past we might have said that babies were "given up." Now we know that women make an active choice, often with the best interest of the baby at heart. Birth mothers and adoptive parents have told us that they prefer to say, "the baby was placed for adoption."

One of the greatest privileges parents have is telling children the story of how they came to be part of a family. The story of how a child comes into a family is central to a sense of belonging. For adopting families this story of "coming home" could include the birth mother or surrogate. Explaining how babies are created is both biological and relational. Telling children how babies come into the world is a story of love and belonging that includes biology, family structure, and faith. Yes, it is a story about bodies, people, sperm, and eggs; it is also a story of God's beautiful creation. It is a story of faith, hope, and love—a story of God working in our lives. Who would want to miss that?

Discussion Questions:

1. What other conversation starters can you design so that you are prepared for the future?
2. What else do you need to learn about human anatomy and sexual reproduction to be prepared for questions?

CHAPTER 25

A FRAMEWORK TO ANSWER QUESTIONS

As parents and teachers, we want to answer children's and teens' questions, but often find that our lack of experience can hinder the conversation. Below is a simple process to answer questions that will keep the conversation on the right track and give you confidence. It is easier than you think—just five steps:

1. Thanks
2. What?
3. Answer
4. Ask
5. Add a faith connection

THANKS

Affirm your child's questions. Say, "Thank you for asking me this question." Sometimes questions come at an inopportune time of the day. Perhaps you are preoccupied or a younger sibling is nearby or you are trying to turn left across four lanes of traffic. Whatever is going on, it is a good idea to take a big, deep breath. Thanking your child helps you catch your breath and gather your thoughts. Often questions are spontaneous and can be a bit of a shock. Saying "thank you" gives you time to switch gears and focus on your child. Verbalizing your appreciation that they asked you conveys that you are profoundly grateful for their trust. Your child could have asked a friend, an older sibling, or even Google.

We are always grateful for the opportunity to connect with our children and learn a little more about their lives and their thoughts and feelings. If you are not in a place where you can answer your child's question, now is the time to say, "I can't answer your question right now. After we put your sister to bed, we will have some quiet time together to talk." Give a reason for not answering the question and give a specific time that you will set aside for a conversation. Affirming the question lays the foundation for open communication.

WHAT

So often the questions children or teens ask are not what they seem. They may remember half a joke, see something written, or hear something on the bus; then they cannot recall accurately what they saw or heard. The second step to answering questions involves taking the time to ask: "What made you think about that?" or "Where did you hear that?" Remember to accept your child's response in a non-judgmental way.

By asking a few clarifying questions, you gain the insight of context. When answering sexuality and faith questions, context can make a significant impact on how to approach the answer.

A parent in one of our workshops wanted some advice on how to answer their daughter's question. The daughter wanted to be a pimp for Halloween. After asking some clarifying questions, the parent discovered the fourth grader wanted to wear sparkling jewelry and flashy clothes. The parent learned that their daughter had been watching the TV show

Pimp My Ride. The parent decided to suggest a gypsy costume or a fancy fairy instead of the pimp. Although the sparkling outfits and extra large necklaces were just the look the child wanted, knowing the context of the question led the parent into a conversation that was relevant to the child's experience rather than into a complicated discussion of prostitution and pimps.

Parents naturally ask, "Where do I start?" or "How much do I tell my teen? I don't want to tell them too much." They are right—too much information can hinder communication rather than enhance it. If you know the context of your child's question and you've identified the question your child is actually asking, you're on the right track.

The next step is to think about the different ways you might approach the question. Do you need to give a simple definition? Is a more in-depth conversation in order? If you need some time to think about all of this, let your child know that you will have a conversation later; then set a time, and keep your commitment.

If, for example, a sixth grader asked, "What is rape?", before answering, the parent could assess whether the child knows about sexual intercourse. Does the teen understand violence? What conversations have they already had that would allow the teen to understand the concept of rape? What familiar concepts can be built upon? Each question your child asks likely has several satisfactory answers. A parent could give a straightforward definition: "Rape is when someone forces someone else to have sexual intercourse." A more basic answer, perhaps for a younger child, would be: "Rape is forcing someone to do something they don't want to do. Rape is a sad thing that hurts." Alternatively, a parent might choose to give a more legally nuanced answer: "Rape is forcing someone to have sexual intercourse against their will. Rape is a crime."

When you think about your answer, be sure to teach relevant skills, if there is an opportunity. Any of the responses above could include some examples of how to say "No" and how to respect a "No" from a friend. Say, "Whenever someone says 'No,' you must listen to that no. 'No' does not mean 'Maybe,' or 'Later,' or even 'Yes.'" With elementary students, parents can practice the concept of "Stop" when wrestling or tickling. When someone says, "Stop," then we stop the game. You are teaching children to respect one another and teaching them that NO means NO every time.

Learn to look for a variety of avenues for answering questions, taking advantage of every opportunity to check in with your children. Parents may choose to start with very basic answers, and expand on their answers in response to cues from their child. Once you decide how to answer a question, give your answer in a neutral tone of voice using age-appropriate vocabulary.

ASK

"Did I answer your question?" This may be the part of the formula most often forgotten, yet it's crucial to communication. Parents sometimes miss the mark when answering questions—that is normal. Even when we have explored the context of the question, we sometimes misinterpret the question and inadvertently go down the wrong road entirely.

Taking time to confirm that the child's question has been answered gives you another opportunity to engage with your child and to make sure that you gave a relevant and helpful response. Keep your posture open and wait for your child's response. After you have answered the original question and any follow-up questions, ask again, "Is this what you needed to talk about?" End the conversation with, "Thank you for coming to me; remember you can ask me anything! I love you and I want to be a part of your journey." By deliberately telling your children that you want them to come to you, you reassert your desire for open communication with your child.

Adolescents and teens will be reminded that you want to be a part of their lives, even the awkward and embarrassing parts. What if the answer was by all reports terrible? You mumbled your words, shook with nervousness, and babbled on too much. Take heart—answering the question and inviting more questions ensures that you will have more opportunities in the future. You probably did a better job than you think. Remember that your teen is new at this as well. You can always go back and re-answer a question, if necessary.

Your nervousness and hesitation will subside as you and your child become more accustomed to talking about faith and bodies.

ADD A FAITH CONNECTION

Attaching a "Faith Connection" to your answer is your opportunity to share your faith and values with your children. Faith Connections are uncomplicated to use because they reflect your faith and your experience with God. They are personal, yet simple. "No matter what happens, I love you and God loves you." "There is nothing that we can ever do that will separate us from God's love." "You are uniquely and wonderfully made!"

Children and teens need to see decision-making processes in action. Sometimes we call these Faith Connections, sometimes values. Whatever you want to call them works, just remember to add them!

Our values are frequently an unspoken part of the processes adults use to make decisions. Teens are already out in the world making important decisions about their friendships, behavior, and their faith. Identifying values and naming them allows children and teens to learn how to make similar decisions in "real life." Attaching values in conversations gives children the foundation they need and a road map for a faith-filled life.

Parents are looking for ways to show children and teens how to walk in faith following the pathway of hope and love. Parents want to teach moral and ethical behavior and sometimes think, in order to do so, they must enforce hard and fast rules for teens to follow. Unfortunately, those rigid rules are sometimes inadequate when teens begin to navigate their complicated, dynamic lives. Margaret Farley in *Just Love* posits that "relationships—with others, ourselves, God—always have moral elements; but the sex or lack of sex in them

Faith Connections are thoughts and feelings about God, the world, people, and actions that you want to teach your children.

may be less genuine moral significance than are the elements such as respect, trust, honesty, fairness and faithfulness."[210]

The world has not even dreamed of so much that your child will encounter and experience. The old rules do not always apply to new technologies and social situations; however, your values and Faith Connections do apply. When hard and fast rules do not help your child in a new situation, the values you teach will. When a teen encounters a novel situation, they will use these values and Faith Connections as their touchstone. The values they have internalized will resonate in their heart and mind and guide them when their parents are not present to lean on.

How do you express Faith Connections and help your child internalize those values? How do you decide which Faith Connections to teach?

Begin by thinking about your own foundational values—the words that help you in difficult situations. Think about the values that your child needs in order to live a faith-filled life. If you only had five things to teach your child, what would you choose? Some parents keep a list of Faith Connections to impart to their children. Check them off as you hear your child or teen express those values in conversations with you. Once they have internalized the value, check it off the list. Then move on to the next value to be learned. Remember you are creating the framework for your child from which their values and faith will spring. Be patient with yourself. Creating value statements takes practice. Try a few value statements and remember to adjust them over time as you continue the conversations with your child.

Below are a few examples of Faith Connections that we have shared with parents, and parents have shared with us, over the years:

- God loves you; that means all of you. Your spirit and your body are beautiful.
- God made a way for families to have babies. Our bodies are perfectly created to make babies.
- God made each of us uniquely different and wonderful. We are made in the image of God.
- You do not have to be like everyone else; you are a unique creation of God.

- God created families to love and care for each other.
- It is a sacred joy to raise a child. I love you and I love being your parent.
- God created sexual intercourse to be an intimate expression of love.
- Sometimes people use what God meant to be good as a way to get their own way or to make them feel better.
- Someone who is selfish thinks only about themself. Whenever we do something thinking only of ourselves, we are being selfish.
- As children of God we are called to love one another as God has loved us.
- Prostitution is an example of exploitation: using someone as an object and in a selfish way without regard to that person's well-being. As children of God we seek to help people who are being exploited (child laborers, underpaid workers, prostitutes) by changing their environments and fighting for justice.
- As followers of Jesus we seek to love others as we love ourselves. That means we should not call anyone names—like faggot, homo, or fairy. Calling people names is never the right thing to do.
- When you are out in the world, you are representing our whole family and me. Remember that you are a child of God and a member of this family. Remembering these things will help you decide what to do.
- Our family will be a place where you are always loved and respected.
- God does not make mistakes and you are one of God's precious creations.
- Christians respect other people. When Christians go out into the world, we seek to respect the dignity of every human being—whether they wear the correct clothes, whether they agree with us, or whether they are cool or nerdy.
- Your body belongs to you. No one should ever make you do anything that makes you feel uncomfortable. If someone

does anything that makes you feel uncomfortable or hurts you, tell an adult immediately. God is glad when you are safe.

- Christians believe that sex and sexuality are both sacred, which is a way of saying it is wonderful, special, and private. This does not mean that you have to keep anything about your sexuality a secret. You can seek God's guidance and talk to people you trust about everything that happens to you as you grow up.
- There is nothing that can ever separate us from God's love. Even though we sometimes make mistakes, God is always with us to help us and forgive us.[211]

The Faith Connections or values that you want to teach may seem overwhelming. Writing a list of values helps to keep parents on track. Of course you can change the list and even check some off as your child internalizes what they hear.

Choose one or two of your own value statements to focus on with your child or teen. Reinforce those values through conversations, attaching them whenever you can. Society teaches our children values through TV, movies, and advertising. Do not be shy or apologize for teaching your values—your voice needs to be heard more frequently than these societal messages.

Let your children know what you believe and what is important to you—often! One day you will hear your growing child tell someone else the values you have been teaching—sometimes they will even correct a parent. Congratulate yourself on a job well done, and move on to another Faith Connection.

TAKE HEART

When a child asks a question about sexuality, it can be challenging to meet them where they are and answer the question directly and honestly. I remember the first time I was caught off guard with a question about the family dog being neutered. I stuttered, stammered, and tried to think of what to say to a terrified child who could not imagine how having testicles removed could ever be a good thing. That conversation was inadequate and bordered on incompetency. In the end, I found myself circling back and giving it another try. Looking back, I can see the value in admitting that I was learning, too, and asking to take a second shot at the question. That vulnerability and honesty built trust between us. The good news is it gets easier with practice. And I was given the opportunity to be a part of the wondering and learning.

It takes courage to practice new skills, even with children. Take heart, remember that your children are a gift from God—you are the caretakers. Their questions are invitations into their lives and opportunities to forge deeper and stronger connections. Take a deep breath and give it a try. Your courage will be rewarded with a knowledgeable, more self-confident child and a stronger relationship.

Discussion Questions:

1. What has worked well for you in your conversations with children about sexuality?
2. What has not worked so well? in your conversations with youth? in your conversations with other adults?
3. How might you improve in any future conversation? What might you need to reflect upon?
4. What has been the toughest question posed to you? In retrospect, how might you have answered it?

CHAPTER 26

THE QUESTION

As parents and educators, we are asked questions all the time. One question parents often dread is the infamous, "Where do babies come from?" And sometimes we are the ones asking the question, "Where did you hear that?" (when children share knowledge of sex). How can these conversations be framed to include a Faith Connection or value? Sometimes it comes down to one question that makes us most nervous. It can come at any age.

WHEN AM I READY TO HAVE SEX?

A person is ready to have sex when they are in the right relationship with someone else, and their spirit, body, mind, and feelings are ready. When I think about whether a person is ready for the responsibility and the consequences of sexual intercourse or oral sex, I think about several things:

> *Are you physically ready?* Is your body ready for sexual activity? Is your body or your partner's body ready to have a baby? Having a child is a natural consequence of sexual

intercourse. Teenaged bodies are not ready to carry a baby for forty weeks. Teenage mothers can have difficulty in labor and delivery. Many babies born to teenagers are premature and have health problems.[212]

Are you emotionally ready? Being intimate and having sexual intercourse connects you with someone in the most personal and private way. Are you ready to be that close to someone? Being sexually active changes your relationship. Are you ready for the new emotions that you might feel?

Is your relationship ready? How would you feel if you broke up with your partner? Can you and your partner talk about anything—even birth control and prevention of disease? Do you want to be sexually active or are you trying to make someone else happy? Can you afford to raise a baby if you or your partner becomes pregnant? How are you caring for and protecting your partner and yourself?

Are you spiritually ready? Would God be smiling knowing that you are honoring the gift of sexuality that you have been given? Does your church say helpful things about sexuality that speak to you? Are there mature Christian friends who say things about sexuality that you might care to hear? Sexual intercourse is best experienced with someone whom you share friendship, commitment, intimacy, and trust. As Christians we naturally recognize God as a part of all of our relationships, including our most intimate relationships. Our choices about our friendships, romantic relationships, and

Faith Connection: Being responsible means understanding the consequences of your actions, thinking through your behavior, and taking adequate steps to be safe. Talk to me or other trusted adults when you are trying to make a difficult decision. Asking, "What would God think about my actions, attitude, and motivations?" can help you make complicated decisions by refocusing your attention on how God calls us to live as Christians.

our bodies are subject to Jesus' commandment: "Love one another as I have loved you."[213]

Is your mind ready? Being sexually active takes planning in order to be safe. How have you planned to stay safe? Will you use birth control and, if so, what type of birth control? How will you protect yourself and your partner from contracting STIs? Who is going to pay for the contraceptive? Are you mature enough to raise a child? If you are not ready to make those decisions, then you are not ready to be sexually active.

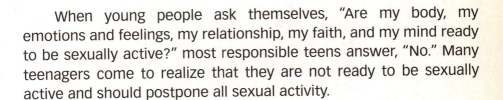

When young people ask themselves, "Are my body, my emotions and feelings, my relationship, my faith, and my mind ready to be sexually active?" most responsible teens answer, "No." Many teenagers come to realize that they are not ready to be sexually active and should postpone all sexual activity.

Discussion Questions:

1. How do you create a safe and open environment for conversations with children or teens about sexuality?
2. How has your faith helped you in your conversations?
3. What is the next step for you in talking about faith and sex in church or at home?

CONCLUSION

CALLED TO BE TRUTH-TELLERS

Engaging in conversations and education about sexuality in the church setting ensures that we respect the place that sexuality has in our lives. Sexuality has an integral place in our lives; as faithful people seeking to follow Christ, the Church has much to say about the ways in which we choose to live our lives. One place to look for the answer is in the New Testament. In his letter to the Ephesians, Paul sets the stage for ways to think about how we walk with others in community.

> Therefore, as a prisoner for the Lord, I encourage you to live as people worthy of the call you received from God. Conduct yourselves with all humility, gentleness, and patience. Accept each other with love, and make an effort to preserve the unity of the Spirit with the peace that ties you together. You are one body and one spirit, just as God also called you in one hope. There is one Lord, one faith, one baptism, and one God and Father of all, who is over all, through all, and in all.[214]

God *begs* us to live a life worthy of our calling. The word "beg" is powerful. The call to a life that is lived in the awareness of our calling is not a suggestion, or a slight mention, but a pleading. The word "beg" demands our attention and our consideration. We get a sense that we are being called back into the life that God has dreamed for us. A life worthy of the giver. A life worthy of being called a gift from God.

Living a life worthy of our calling means bringing our very best selves into our relationship with God and with others. We are called into a life of community, into a covenant with God through Jesus Christ. Our response to that high calling is to bring the self that God created, the unmasked, and undefended self. Richard Rohr calls this "our True Self."[215] We could also call it our soul.

Setting our faith in this context—a faith lived in the light of a life worthy of our calling—gives us the opportunity to ask what would a life worthy of our calling look like? What would it mean for our relationships to each other and to ourselves?

What if knowing that we were capable of a covenant relationship with God, we chose to love and forgive others and ourselves? What if we were able to let go of the actions and choices that we judged as "bad" and looked for God in our present lives? As sexual beings it would mean understanding and accepting our need for each other: our needs to connect, create, and sustain intimacy.

Dr. Brené Brown's research into vulnerability and shame points to our need for connection. We are "hardwired for connection."[216] The hardwiring is at our very core. Our need for connection and intimacy is the call to life lived in community. We must recognize that the joy experienced in that intimacy sustains us through our own development of faith, hope, and love.

Although intimacy can be a physical expression, it is not always expressed through sex. As sexual beings, we must recognize that intimacy is carried in the body *and* soul. We are a people who are born and living in our bodies, called to follow Christ into this deeper relationship with God and each other. We are people born into bodies. We cannot live in separation from our bodies. Embracing our embodiment requires an expansive view of our bodies. When someone is in pain, we naturally reach out to them. We seek to connect through

> **Intimacy** is the deep expression of connection and love that God calls us to draw ever closer to people.

touch, to love through our physical presence. How often do we respond with reaching out to hug a friend or squeeze a hand?

Living a life worthy of our calling means seeking a deeper transformational life, recognizing God in all aspects of our lives. Treating others and ourselves with dignity and respect would be a first in living a life of spiritual abundance.

Once we see that we are called to live a life that is worthy of God's calling, we seek to recognize our True Selves and the True Self of those we love. The expression of our sexuality is connected to our desire to live this holy life. Who we love and how we love does matter. When we begin to see our sexuality in new avenues of gender, attraction, and expression, we open the doors for self-acceptance and grace born of divine love.

The Church can be a place that offers people the grace and space that they need to openly explore the questions of gender, attraction, and sexual expression. The Church is the expression of Christ's love for us. To grow together in Christ's love, we must demonstrate radical hospitality to all people, including those who identify differently. First, we must modernize our church programs and the language we use, if we are to create an environment in which each and every person is welcomed into Christ's love as they are.

When we are able to celebrate each other and ourselves as we are, we can say we are living lives worthy of our calling. As people of faith, responding to the imperative to live a life worthy of our calling encompasses our whole lives and our whole person as we seek to live in an open, grace-filled community. It is a calling that is fulfilled throughout our lives—from birth to death.

PART V

RESOURCES

THE *THESE ARE OUR BODIES* PROGRAM

This book, *These Are Our Bodies: Sexuality & Faith at Church & Home*, is the foundation book for a human sexuality program published by Church Publishing Incorporated. Modules for a variety of age levels will be offered, with the first being a Middle School module published simultaneously with this volume. Middle school (ages 11–13) is when most parents (and churches) seek assistance in talking with young people about sexuality, hence our beginning with this age level. However, we believe that all ages and stages need to be always cognizant of our sexuality in terms of our faith and life.

The *These Are Our Bodies* program is a comprehensive faith and sexuality program that can be used in a variety of settings including Sunday morning classes, evening events, or seminars taught over a Friday afternoon and Saturday. It can also be used in home or school settings. The program is based on the universal needs of young people and their parents. In order to honor and lift up parents as the primary sexuality educators to their children, parents are an integral part of the program.

Developmentally appropriate and creatively interactive, this faith-based approach to sexuality places human sexuality in the context of faith. Direct and indirect teaching around concepts such as God's creation, scripture, and sexuality as gifts from God are intertwined throughout the sessions. Conversations and teaching around the stewardship of gifts, responsible behavior, and God's grace and love abound in this program. The sessions in *These Are Our Bodies* program materials (age-based *Leader Guide, Parent Book,* and *Participant Book*) are each designed to teach concepts that make a connection between faith and sexuality through the modeling of facilitator and small-group leader interaction, how to answer questions, and how to create a safe, learning atmosphere.

All children need reassurance that their growing and developing is normal and expected. As they continue their journey toward adulthood and independence, the Church can provide the environment and opportunities to bridge the gap between their everyday lives and their faith lives. They need to know there is a place for them to ask their questions and receive honest answers.

In 1982 the Task Force on Human Sexuality and Family Life Education was created as part of The Episcopal Church's Education for Mission and Ministry Unit. They developed a program titled *Sexuality: A Divine Gift.* The following is taken from its Foreword, as we believe it continues to be relevant and represents the intentions of *These Are Our Bodies* as well:

> The program presented invites you to join in exploring this vital area of human existence, where, we believe, no one has all the answers; rather it is an opportunity to share unique lessons learned from our collective experiences. Sharing these experiences in the manner described in this manual is expected to evoke both growth and new insights for those who participate.
>
> The program is *theological* in asking participants to bring their involvement in this program all they know and have experienced of God as they reflect on contemporary living. The involvement is *experiential* and *dialogue centered* in asking participants to share the wisdom they all possess.
>
> It is *intergenerational* and *holistic* in seeking to gather together those from each generation: married and single persons; bonded, with varying relationships. It is *comprehensive* in asking everyone to consider a variety of

role models and living patterns which are emulated whether a person lives in a city, suburban, or rural environment and whether or not a person sees him or herself as a participant in the mainstream of society.[217]

GOALS

The program teaches that we are all God's children—loved and redeemed. Each of us is made in the image of God—good and holy. There is nothing that we can do to separate us from the love of God. Forgiveness and grace are gifts given to each of us and are born from God's love for us. Human beings are imperfect. As people still under construction, we are in need of and beneficiaries of God's redeeming grace. We are best when we are open, vulnerable, and truthful with each other. These messages are embedded in the way that facilitators and small-group leaders offer answers to questions and interact with the young people.

As children and adolescents continue their journey toward adulthood and independence, the church can provide the environment and opportunities to bridge the gap between the everyday life and the faith lives of our children and youth, as well as ourselves as adults. The use of prayer and scripture to discuss themes around sexuality is core.

The second goal of the program is to give participants the experiences and opportunities to explore sexuality in the context of their faith. Each participant book will guide them to reflect on what they are learning and make faith connections. As topics around sexuality are introduced, taught, and discussed, the facilitators and small-group leaders will continually connect that new knowledge with skills that can be used in everyday life. The discussions and questions covered make a concrete connection to our faith.

Depending on age appropriateness, topics will include: self-image, love, friendship, biological sex, gender identity and expression, romantic and sexual attraction, refusal skills, prostitution and pornography, cyber bullying, sexually transmitted infections, abstinence and birth control, assertive and aggressive behavior, facts and fiction around sexuality, media (such as the Internet, advertising, movies, music), decision-making, listening skills, and value clarification.

The third goal is to empower parents as the primary sexuality educators of their children. The best way to help families to make the connection between faith and sexuality is by inviting children, teens, and parents to learn and share within the context of a faith community. As a parent, it can be very difficult to address issues around puberty, development, and sexuality in a few conversations. The issues children and teens face and the questions they have are biological, social, spiritual, cognitive, and emotional. The joint sessions with participants and parents give families the time and space to explore a wide range of issues together.

In keeping with the goal of empowering parents as the primary educators of their children, age-appropriate information is shared with all (parents and participants). Participants are encouraged to ask their parents questions and enter into conversations with them about the thoughts, feelings, and questions with which they are wrestling. Recognizing that there can be a wide range of beliefs and opinions about some controversial topics even at church, we seek to empower all parents to effectively teach their children about faith and sexuality. A portion of the parent program is devoted to helping parents clarify values and communicate those values and faith connections to their children, as they answer questions about difficult or sensitive topics.

GLOSSARY

Authors' note: Many of these definitions were adapted from The Trevor Project, Planned Parenthood, Just Communities, and Trans Student Educational Resources.

abstinence: The self-imposed practice of not doing something that a person wants to do. Sexual abstinence is the choice not to participate in some (or all) sexual activities. Someone may choose abstinence for any number of reasons: moral, religious, not feeling ready, to prevent sexually transmitted infections or pregnancy, and many more.

adolescence: The period in human growth and development that occurs after childhood and before adulthood, from ages ten to nineteen. It represents one of the critical transitions in life and is characterized by tremendous growth and change that is second only to that of infancy. Biological processes drive many aspects of this growth and development, with the onset of puberty marking the passage from childhood to adolescence.

affirmed female: Someone who identifies as female but was labeled male at birth.

affirmed male: Someone who identifies as male but was labeled female at birth.

agape: Unconditional love of the other.

agender: An adjective describing a person who is internally ungendered or does not feel a sense of gender identity.

ally: Someone who supports and stands up for the rights and dignity of individuals and identity groups other than their own. Someone who rejects the dominant ideology and takes action against oppression out of the belief that eliminating oppression will benefit all people in both privilege and target groups.

anorexia: A person with anorexia nervosa may have an intense fear of gaining weight or getting fat. It is one of a number of eating disorders, including bulimia nervosa, in which one who is intensely afraid of gaining weight may eat large amounts of food in a short period of time (a binge) and then eliminate the food and calories by vomiting, using laxatives, diuretics, or diet pills to purge the calories.

asexual: An adjective describing people who form meaningful emotional and spiritual connections, but do not experience sexual attraction to others.

asexuality: Having little to no interest in having sex, even though one may desire emotionally intimate relationships. Asexual people are also known as "Ace" or "Aces." Within the ace community there are many ways for people to identify.

Baptismal Covenant, the: The promises made between God, the baptized, and God's people during the liturgy of Holy Baptism. The promises require that we renounce Satan, repent of our sins, and accept Jesus as our Lord and Savior as well as answer other questions with "I will with God's help." For infants, their parents and sponsors make promises to support the baptized in their journey within the Church, to know Christ, and be able to follow him.

binary: Used as an adjective to describe the genders female/male or woman/man.

biological sex: How we are defined as female, male, or intersex. It describes our internal and external bodies, including our sexual and reproductive anatomy, our genetic makeup, and our hormones.

birth control: Any method used to prevent pregnancy, including, but not limited to: condoms, IUDs, birth control pills, the rhythm method, vasectomy, and tubal ligation.

bisexual/bisexuality: An umbrella term for people who experience sexual and/or emotional attraction to more than one gender (pansexual, fluid, omnisexual, queer).

body image: The way you see yourself, imagine how you look, and feel about your body.

cisgender: An adjective describing someone who identifies with the gender they were given at birth. Most people who have female bodies feel like girls or women, and most people who have male bodies feel like boys or men. Derived from the Latin word meaning "on the same side." "Cisgender" does not indicate biology, gender expression, or sexuality/sexual orientation. **Cis** is not a "fake" word and is not a slur. (Note: Cisgender does not have an "ed" at the end).

consent: An agreement between participants to engage in sexual activity.

covenant: A contract or agreement, such as between God and God's people. The New Covenant is the new relationship with God given by Jesus Christ, the Messiah, to the apostles; and, through them, to all who believe in him. (BCP, p. 850)

cross-dresser: A term to describe someone who dresses in clothes typical of the opposite sex but does not necessarily live as the sex. A more normative and preferred term than "transvestite."

cyber bullying: Bullying that takes place using electronic technology including devices and equipment such as cell phones, computers, and tablets as well as communication tools including social media sites, text messages, chat, and websites. Examples include mean text messages or e-mails, rumors sent by e-mail or posted on social networking sites, and embarrassing pictures, videos, websites, or fake profiles.

eros: Physical love and sexual desire.

friendship: The connecting bond of affection between people. It is loyal, respectful, mutual, and committed.

gay: A man who is attracted to other men often calls himself gay or homosexual.

gender: Society's expectations about how we should think and act as girls and boys, and women and men. It is our biological, social, and legal status as women and men.

gender affirming surgery: Surgery does not change one's sex or gender, only one's genitalia. Also known today as genital reconstruction surgery and genital reassignment surgery. The terms "sex change," "sex reassignment surgery," and "gender reassignment surgery" are considered inaccurate and offensive.

gender binary: A traditional understanding that one is either male or female based on one's chromosomal sex (XX – female/ XY – male). This system is oppressive to anyone who defies their sex assigned at birth, but particularly those who are gender-variant or do not fit neatly into one of the two standard categories.

gender expression: How one conveys their gender and gender roles through clothing, behavior, and personal appearance.

gender fluid: An adjective describing an individual who does not have an internal sense that they are a man or a woman.

gender identity: One's perception of the social category to which they belong, for example being male, female, neither, or both. For example, a person can have a penis and testicles but not the internal sense that they are a man. That individual's gender identity might be described as female.

gender roles: Society's set of roles, values, and expectations for what it means to be a girl/woman or a boy/man in a particular culture. Gender roles vary from culture to culture and over time. The United States culture recognizes two distinct gender roles. One is the "masculine" (having the qualities of characteristics attributed to males.) The other is the "feminine" (having the qualities or characteristics attributed to females). In other words, this is what we learn from our culture about what a "real man" or a "real woman" is supposed to be/do. A third gender role, rarely condoned in our society, is androgyny combining assumed male *(andro)* and female *(gyne)* qualities. Note: There are also gender roles around non-binary genders.

genderqueer: An adjective used to describe a person who is part of a group of people who do not feel that they fit into either of the traditional two genders of a gender-binary system. As with any other group that aligns with transgender identities, the reasons for identifying as genderqueer vary.

Gender Unicorn, the: A friendly looking purple creature complete with rainbow thought bubble and a pair of hearts on its chest developed by Trans Student Educational Resources. Alongside the Unicorn is a chart to educate readers on emotional and sexual attraction as well as gender identity, expression, and assignment.

heterosexuality: People who are attracted to people of other genders often call themselves heterosexual or straight.

homosexuality: Romantic attraction, sexual attraction, or sexual behavior between members of the same sex or gender. A woman who is attracted to other women often calls herself gay, lesbian, or homosexual. A man who is attracted to other men often calls himself gay or homosexual.

hospitality: To welcome and love the stranger as you would your own family.

Imago Dei: Image of God, denoting the symbolic relation between God and humanity.

intersex: An adjective describing a person with a less common combination of hormones, chromosomes, and anatomy that are used to assign sex at birth. It is a group of conditions where there is discrepancy between the external genitals and the internal genitals (the testes and ovaries). Although many people are unaware, about 1 in 2,000 people born in the United States can be defined as "intersex."[218] Many intersex people are given a sex of male or female at birth, even if they fall somewhere in the middle. In the past, parents of intersex newborns picked one sex for the child either through an operation or hormone treatment or a combination. Sometimes intersex characteristics aren't noticed until puberty, when our body goes through a lot of different changes. Remember, sex does not equal gender; it's an entirely different set of determinants that relates to our biology and physical characteristics. Generally we think about sex as a binary: male and female. However, there are several conditions that a person can be born with that don't fit the typical definitions of female or male. For example, a person might be born appearing to be female on the outside, but have mostly male anatomy on the inside. Or a person may be born with genitals that seem to be in-between the usual male and female types. (Note: The word *hermaphrodite* is an archaic term from Greek mythology. It is offensive to intersex people.)

lesbian: A woman who is attracted to other women often calls herself gay, lesbian, or homosexual.

LGBTQ+: A collection of identities short for lesbian, gay, bisexual, transgender, queer, questioning, intersex, asexual, aromantic, pansexual. An inclusive term that seeks to capture all sexual and gender identities other than heterosexual. Sometimes this acronym is replaced with "queer." (Note: "Ally" is not included in the acronym by most.)

love: A mature love includes acceptance, non-judgment, and a commitment to help another person grow emotionally and spiritually, a love that respects the dignity of another person. There are many aspects of love. See also: *agape, eros, philia, storge*.

marriage: The legal and religious lifelong union between two people who make their vows before God and the Church and receive the grace and blessing of God to help them fulfill their vows. (BCP, p. 861)

meaning-making: The defining of a concept outside of oneself.

Millennials: Those born in the 80s, 90s, and early 2000s. As with any generation there is flexibility as to the specific-year boundaries for Millennials.

moral identity: The importance of moral ideals, traits, and actions to a person's sense of identity.

mosaic genetics: The presence of two or more populations of cells with different genotypes in one individual who has developed from a single fertilized egg; some of their cells have XX chromosomes and some have XY. See also **intersex**.

mutuality: Respect, caring, and equitable sharing of power and resources between people.

non-binary sexual orientation: A way to describe attractions to people who do not identify as just male/man or female/woman. Examples of non-binary sexual orientations include, but are not limited to: pansexual, bisexual, queer. These terms often mean different things to different people, and that's okay! Make sure to ask questions and be respectful when learning about what each label means for each person.

Nones: The growing number of Americans, particularly in the Millennial generation, who say they do not belong to any organized faith.

pansexual: ("pan") A person who is attracted to multiple or all types of people, no matter what their sex or gender might be. Also an adjective referring to such people. This term is being used more frequently as more people acknowledge that gender is not binary.

philia: friendship, fondness.

polysexual: People who are attracted to more than one gender or sex but do not wish to identify as bisexual because it implies that there are only two binary genders or sexes. Also an adjective referring to such people.

prostitutes/prostitution: People who are paid to perform sexual acts.

puberty: The physiological, emotional, and cognitive process that occurs in early adolescents as children grow into adults.

purity: Refers to someone's virginity and their abstinence from sexual activity.

queer: Someone who does not identify as straight and/or does not identify as cisgender; a non-binary label that describes diverse gender identities and sexual orientations. The word queer can also be used as a way to reject the acronym "LGBT," which some people feel is restricting. There is a lot of overlap between queer and trans identities, but not all queer people are trans and not all trans people are queer. The word queer is still sometimes used as a hateful slur, so although it has been mostly reclaimed, be careful with its use.

questioning: To be unsure or less certain of your sexual orientation. You can also be questioning about your gender identity. People figure out their sexuality and gender identity at different points in their lives, and there's no wrong way to identify.

refusal skills: The ability and learned techniques to assertively say "no" to sexual advances.

romantic attraction: Attraction that makes people desire romantic contact or interaction with another person or persons.

romantic orientation: Describes an individual's pattern of romantic attraction based on a person's gender(s) regardless of one's sexual orientation. For individuals who experience sexual attraction, their sexual orientation and romantic orientation are often in alignment (they experience sexual attraction toward individuals of the same gender(s) as the individuals they are interested in forming romantic relationships with).

self-image: The way one views their abilities, appearance, and intelligence as well as who and what they are.

sexual: Of or relating to sex, sexuality, physiological processes.

sexual attraction: Attraction that makes people desire sexual contact or show sexual interest in another person(s).

sexual harassment: Includes unwelcome sexual advances, requests for sexual favors, and other verbal, non-verbal, or physical conduct of a sexual or gender-based nature. Sexual violence is a form of sexual harassment and is a crime that must be reported to law enforcement.

sexual intercourse: Sexual activity between two people, especially penetration of the vagina, anus, or mouth.

sexual orientation: A person's enduring physical, emotional, romantic, and/or other form of attraction to others (male or female). Sexual orientation involves a person's feelings and sense of identity; it may or may not be evident in the person's appearance or behavior. People may have attractions to people of the same or opposite sex, but may elect not to act on these feelings.

sexuality: "... a central aspect of being human throughout life encompasses sex, gender identities and roles, sexual orientation, eroticism, pleasure, intimacy, and reproduction. Sexuality is experienced and expressed in thoughts, fantasies, desires, beliefs, attitudes, values, behaviors, practices, roles, and relationships. While sexuality can include all of these dimensions, not all of them are always experienced or expressed. Sexuality is influenced by the interaction of biological, psychological, social, economic, political, cultural, legal, historical, religious, and spiritual factors."[219]

sexually transmitted infections (STIs): Infections that are spread primarily through person-to-person sexual contact including vaginal, anal, and oral sex. STIs can also be spread through non-sexual means via blood or blood products such as needles. Several, in particular HIV and syphilis, can also be transmitted from mother to child during pregnancy and childbirth, and through blood products and tissue transfer. A person can have an STI without having obvious symptoms of disease. Common symptoms of STIs include vaginal discharge, urethral discharge or burning in men, genital ulcers, and abdominal pain. There are more than thirty different sexually transmissible bacteria, viruses, and parasites. The most common infections are gonorrhea, chlamydial infection, syphilis, trichomoniasis, chancroid, genital herpes, genital warts, human immunodeficiency virus (HIV) infection, and hepatitis B infection. While all these infections are treatable, there is no cure for genital herpes, genital warts, and HIV.

storge: Familial love, like that between a parent and child.

trans/transgender: The "T" in LGBTQ+. Derived from the Latin word meaning "across from" or "on the other side of." Some people have a gender identity that does not match up with their biological sex. For example, they were born with "female" sex organs (vulva, vagina, uterus), but they feel like a male. People in this community sometimes call themselves transgender or trans. Trans can also include people who do not identify with the strict male/female gender roles the world tells us we should fit into. Sometimes people who do not feel either male or female call themselves genderqueer. (Note: Terms like transgender*ed*, *tranny*, or, *he-she* are old-fashioned and hurtful.) See also:

transition: A person's process of developing and assuming a gender expression to match their gender identity. Transition can include: coming out to one's family, friends, and/or co-workers; changing one's name and/or sex on legal documents; hormone therapy; and possibly (though not always) some form of surgery. It's best not to assume how one transitions as it is different for everyone.

transvestite: A term that has fallen out of favor and has been replaced by **cross-dresser**, to describe one who dresses in clothes typical of the opposite sex but does not necessarily live as that sex.

Two Spirit: A third gender recognized in indigenous cultures as someone who identified with both male and female gender roles, feeling that their body simultaneously manifested both a masculine and feminine balance of spirit. Today it is an umbrella term used to describe various indigenous gender identities in North America, including intersecting oppressions (race, colonialism, queerness, sexuality, and transgenderism). It is a culturally specific term that cannot be transferred into other cultures.

WEBSITES

GENERAL INFORMATION AND EDUCATION

Advocates for Youth: Helps young people in making informed and responsible decisions about their reproductive and sexual health; offers lessons and curricula. www.advocatesforyouth .org/sex-education-home.

The Coalition for Positive Sexuality: Offers information in English and Spanish for young people who are sexually active or considering sexual activity. http://positive.org.

Gender Unicorn: A graphic designed by Landyn Pan and Anna Moore and developed by Trans Student Educational Services to portray the distinction between gender, sex assigned at birth, and sexuality. It includes a continuum of gender identity, gender expression, sex assigned at birth, physical attraction, and emotional attraction, understanding that every individual places themselves on various points along the spectrum. www.transstudent.org/gender.

GLADD: Begun in 1985 and originally known as the "Gay & Lesbian Alliance Against Defamation," this organization works with print, broadcast, and online news sources to bring people powerful stories from the LGBT community that build support for equality. Their site includes a resources list in these categories: political, bisexual, youth, military, transgender, aging, legal, and general. www.glaad.org.

GLSEN (Gay, Lesbian & Straight Education Network): Provides resources for incorporating LGBT history, themes, and people by providing lesson plans, curriculum, and ways to encourage respectful behavior, critical thinking and social justice in the classroom. Also offers model policies for the inclusion of LGBTQIA persons in public schools. www.glsen.org and www.glsen.org/blog.

Iwannaknow: For youth who desire to learn about sexual health to make healthy decisions. www.iwannaknow.org.

Just Communities: Located in Santa Barbara, California, brings together diverse community members and empowers them to be leaders who promote equality around issues of race, socio-economic class, sexual orientation, gender identity, age, language, ability, and other identities. Their resources are in English and Spanish. Their executive director, with others, is the founder and copyright owner of the *Genderbread Person* image. www.just-communities.org.

The Kinsey Institute: Works toward advancing sexual health and knowledge worldwide. For more than sixty years, the institute has been a trusted source for investigating and informing the world about critical issues in sex, gender, and reproduction. Their site offers a comprehensive list of data, research, and resources. www.kinseyinstitute.org.

PFLAG (Parents, Families, Friends, and Allies United with LGBTQ People): Founded in 1972 with the simple act of a mother publicly supporting her gay son, PFLAG is the nation's largest family and ally organization. Uniting people who are lesbian, gay, bisexual, transgender, and queer (LGBTQ) with families, friends, and allies, PFLAG is committed to advancing equality and full societal affirmation of LGBTQ people through its threefold mission of support, education, and advocacy. PFLAG has over 400 chapters and 200,000 members and supporters crossing multiple generations of American families in major urban centers, small cities, and rural areas in all 50 states. http://community.pflag.org.

Planned Parenthood: For nearly one hundred years, Planned Parenthood has promoted a common sense approach to women's health and well-being, based on respect for each individual's right to make informed, independent decisions about health, sex, and family planning. Site also includes a webpage of info for teens, tools for parents, and tools for educators. www.plannedparenthood.org.

Search Institute: An organization pioneered in 1958 using social science research to understand the lives, beliefs, and values of young people. Search Institute studies and works to strengthen the Developmental Relationships that help young people acquire the Developmental Assets that are reinforced by Developmental Communities where young people's success is everyone's top priority. www.search-institute.org.

SexEd Library: An online resource for free curriculum and lesson plans. Curriculum is easy to sort through by topic and every lesson is labeled for its age appropriateness. From SEICUS: www.sexedlibrary.org/.

Sex Etc: Provides peer-to-peer education and communication through their website and a magazine. It is a comprehensive sex education website that provides honest and accurate sexual health information. http://sexetc.org/.

Sexuality Information and Education Council of the United States (SIECUS): Provides fact-based sexuality information through publications, websites, trainings, and other resources. As an organization it is recognized as a leader in the field of sexuality and sexuality education and resources for professionals, parents, and the public. Multiple information can be found under the headings: Information & Education, Policy & Advocacy, Newsroom, and Other Resources on the website. www.siecus.org.

Teaching Tolerance: A magazine, website, and other resources produced by the Southern Poverty Law Center, a non-profit organization that combats hate, intolerance, and discrimination through education and litigation. Education materials, movie and book reviews, and free curricular materials for teachers are available. www.tolerance.org. (The Summer 2015 issue of *Teaching Tolerance* featured sexuality topics such as sexual orientation, gender identity, and gender expression. www.tolerance.org/sites/default/files/Teaching%20Tolerance%2050.pdf.)

Trans Student Educational Resources (TSER): A youth-led organization dedicated to transforming the educational environment for trans and gender non-conforming students through advocacy and empowerment. In addition to creating a more trans-friendly education system, their mission is to educate the public and teach trans activists how to be effective organizers. TSER believes that justice for trans and gender non-conforming youth is contingent on an intersectional framework of activism. Ending oppression is a long-term process that can only be achieved through collaborative action. They are the originators of the Gender Unicorn. www.transstudent.org.

The Trevor Project: In addition to providing a 24-hour hotline for teens, especially those who are LGBTQ+ and might be suicidal, their site offers a number of educational resources for youth as well as adults. www.thetrevorproject.org.

FAITH ORGANIZATIONS

The Center for Lesbian & Gay Studies in Religion and Ministry: Has a mission to advance the well-being of lesbian, gay, bisexual, queer, and transgender people and to transform faith communities and the wider society by taking a leading role in shaping a new public discourse on religion, gender identity, and sexuality through education, research, community building, and advocacy. http://clgs.org.

Integrity USA: An organization "proclaiming God's inclusive love in and through The Episcopal Church since 1975." www.integrityusa.org.

National Study of Youth & Religion: A research project (2001–2015) directed by Christian Smith, Professor in the Department of Sociology at the University of Notre Dame and Lisa Pearce, Assistant Professor of Sociology at the University of North Carolina at Chapel Hill. The project was designed to enhance our understanding of the religious lives of American youth from adolescence into young adulthood, using telephone survey and in-depth methods. http://youthandreligion.nd.edu/.

Religious Institute: A multifaith organization dedicated to advocating for sexual health, education, and justice in faith communities and societies. www.religiousinstitute.org.

TransEpiscopal: A group of transgender Episcopalians and their significant others, families, friends, and allies dedicated to enriching the spiritual lives of those who are transgender. Part of their mission is to make The Episcopal Church a welcoming and empowering place that all can truly call our spiritual home. An informal group meeting mostly through the Internet and, though many members are affiliated with The Episcopal Church, TransEpiscopal has no official relationship to The Episcopal Church.

HEALTH CARE

Get Yourself Tested: For a generation accustomed to communicating in shorthand, the GYT acronym presents STD testing in a context that is familiar and relatable to young people. Serving as the information hub for the campaign, this site provides the facts on STDs, testing, and protection; talking tips to help young people communicate with their partners, parents, and health care providers; and a testing center locator provided by the CDC. Resources specifically for health care providers also address common misconceptions that young people have about STDs and testing. Begun in 2009, GYT was developed out of the It's Your (Sex) Life campaign. http://GYTNOW.org.

It's Your (Sex) Life: A public information campaign to support young people in making responsible decisions about their sexual health. The campaign focuses on reducing unintended pregnancy, preventing the spread of sexually transmitted diseases (STDs), including HIV/AIDS, and open communication with partners and health care providers. IYSL was launched in 1997 with the Kaiser Family Foundation. IYSL has been credited with helping to significantly decrease teen pregnancies and increase STD testing in the United States in recent years; the campaign has reached over 200 million young people on the sexual health issues since its inception. www.itsyoursexlife .com.

KidsHealth: Four sites in one: sections for parents, kids, teens, and educators. In addition to the facts about health, it is part of The Nemours Foundation's Center for Children's Health Media, providing families with perspective, advice, and comfort about a wide range of physical, emotional, and behavioral issues that affect children and teens. Complex medical information is given in language that readers can understand and use. All articles, animations, games, and other content go through a rigorous medical review by pediatricians and other medical experts. Ongoing, scheduled medical reviews ensure that the information is as up-to-date as possible. http://kidshealth.org/.

ONLINE AND VIDEO SEX EDUCATION PROGRAMS

For the Bible Tells Me So (2008): Winner of the Audience Award for Best Documentary at the Seattle International Film Festival, Dan Karslake's documentary reconciles homosexuality and biblical scripture, and in the process reveals that Church-sanctioned anti-gay bias is based solely upon a significant (and often malicious) misinterpretation of the bible. As the film notes, most Christians live their lives today without feeling obliged to kill anyone who works on the

Sabbath or eats shrimp. Through the experience of five very normal, very Christian, very American families—including those of former House Majority Leader Richard Gephardt and Episcopal Bishop Gene Robinson—we discover how insightful people of faith handle the realization of having a gay child. With commentary by such respected voices as Bishop Desmond Tutu, Harvard's Peter Gomes, Orthodox Rabbi Steve Greenberg, and Reverend Jimmy Creech. 99 minutes (adult audience) www.forthebibletellsmeso.org.

How Can I Be Sure God Loves Me, Too?: A sermon by the Reverend Mel White, Justice Minister of the UFMCC (Mennonite), in which he offers assurance of God's love for LGBTQ+ people who continue to struggle from the ill-effects of bible abuse. Video via Soul Force; dated but still effective. 23 minutes in three parts (adult audience) www.commonword .ca/ResourceView/6/12400.

Sex +: Founder Laci Green is a sex education activist living in the San Francisco Bay Area. In response to what she believed to be a nationwide failure to provide comprehensive sex education and to adopt healthy, realistic attitudes about sexuality, she launched a YouTube channel (home of Sex Plus) that now features a biweekly video series, a daily blog, and a university lecture circuit. Her focus is on healthy sexual education, feminism, sex positivity, and healthy body image. www .lacigreen.tv

Sex Needs a New Metaphor: A TED Talk from Al Vernacchio, a sexuality educator and author of *For Goodness Sex: Changing the Way We Talk to Teens about Sexuality, Values, and Health* (New York: Harper Wave, 2014) teaches at Friends' Central, a private Quaker school just outside Philadelphia. His positive, enthusiastic and often humorous approach to comprehensive sexuality education (rather than abstinence-only education) has made "Mr. V." a popular speaker. www.ted.com/talks/ al_vernacchio_sex_needs_a_new_metaphor_here_s_one? language=en.

BULLYING AND VIOLENCE

Faith Trust Institute: A national, multifaith, multicultural, training and education organization that works to end sexual and domestic violence. www.faithtrustinstitute.org.

RAINN (Rape, Abuse, & Incest National Network): The nation's largest anti-sexual violence organization, it created and operates the National Sexual Assault Hotline (800.656. HOPE and online.rainn.org.) in partnership with more than 1,100 local sexual assault service providers across the country and operates the Department of Defense's Safe Helpline (www.safehelpline.org.). In 2015, the Online Hotline expanded to offer services in Spanish at rainn.org/es. RAINN also carries out programs to prevent sexual violence, help victims, and ensure that rapists are brought to justice. https://rainn.org/.

Stop Bullying: Information, videos, lessons, and more to respond to bullying. www.stopbullying.gov.

ThinkB4YouSpeak Campaign: A program sponsored by GLSEN and the American Ad Council to assist educators and others who work with teens to introduce the ThinkB4YouSpeak campaign that includes resources, a frame to discuss the ads, and extend learning about the negative consequences of homophobic language and anti-LGBT bias. The core of the guide consists of discussion questions for exploring and analyzing the video, audio, and print ads followed by six educational activities that increase awareness and knowledge of the issues, develop skills for addressing them, and promote social action. YouTube videos support the activities. www.glsen.org/participate/programs/thinkb4youspeak.

TECHNOLOGY AND INTERNET RESOURCES

Common Sense Media: A trusted media education resource offers questions and answers regarding privacy and the

Internet. www.commonsensemedia.org/privacy-and-internet-safety.

Connect Safely: Dedicated to teaching users of online technology about privacy, safety, and security. www.connectsafely.org.

Enough Is Enough: Offers age-based guidelines for the use of the Internet for two- to eighteen-year-olds. www .internetsafety101.org/agebasedguidlines.htm.

Safe Kids: Founded by Larry Magid of ConnectSafely .org, a longtime technology journalist, this site is dedicated to Internet safety for all ages. Also includes "pledges" for kids, teens, and parents about using the Internet. www.safekids .com.

ANNOTATED EDUCATION AND PROGRAM RESOURCES

Beaumont, Jenny and Abbi Long. *These Are Our Bodies: Talking About Faith & Sex at Church & Home—Middle School*. New York: Church Publishing, 2016.

This sexuality education resource from an Episcopal prospective aids the adult reader/teacher/parent in learning and using skills that enable them to embrace and affirm the wholeness of sexuality and to talk openly and honestly about the connection of sexuality and faith with middle-schoolers. Session plans address facts about sexuality, vocabulary, decision-making, faith and daily life, respect, growth and change, behavior, responsibility, values, prayer, and intentionality in an age-appropriate manner for young people. A Leader Guide, Parent Book, and Participant Book offer ten session plans with activities. Additional modules for other age groups will be part of this program in future years.

Our Whole Lives: Lifespan Sexuality Education. Boston: Unitarian Universalist Association of Congregations, 2000.

Designed for multiple age groups, the curriculum itself represents the authors' beliefs about sexuality education as a lifelong process. Three overarching aims are respect, relationships, and responsibility. The curriculum works toward a number of specific goals related to the aims that support children, parents, and the parent/child relationship.

Payne, Elizabeth C. *Youth Ministry in the Age of AIDS 2.* New York: Domestic and Foreign Missionary Society, 2004.

Though dated, this resource was developed in response to the General Convention in 2000 (Resolution A046) to assist young people, Christian educators, and youth leaders to offer HIV education in the context of faith. While the statistics may no longer be accurate, the information and activities are still relevant for today. Now available via the National Episcopal AIDS Coalition for download: www.neac.org/files/documents/youthministryintheageofaids2.pdf.

Reis, Elizabeth. *FLASH Lesson Plans: Comprehensive Sexuality Education Curriculum.* Seattle: Public Health Department of Seattle & King County, 2005.

Family Life and Sexual Health (FLASH) is a science-based, comprehensive sexuality education, public school curriculum designed for elementary through high school. It is an excellent example of a comprehensive sexual health education curriculum. www.kingcounty.gov/healthservices/health/personal/famplan/educators/FLASH.aspx.

Ritchie, James H. *Created By God: Tweens, Faith, and Human Sexuality.* Nashville: Abingdon Press, 2009.

Focuses on God's desire for us to live in intimate relationship with God and each other. The image of Jesus as a 12-year-old boy as told in the Gospel of Luke models tweens' ability for an intimate relationship with God. Designed for fifth and sixth graders, female and male students meet together with parents and small-group leaders over the course of six weeks or a weekend. This curriculum provides comprehensive, step-by-step instructions supporting the coordinator in developing the program. Lesson plans provide clear conversation points and information to small-group leaders. While deeply steeped in

Methodist theology, the curriculum is an easy-to-use product with clear measures, instructions, and materials for students and leaders.

Roberto, John, editor. *Living Well: Christian Practices for Everyday Life.* Naugatuck, CT: Lifelong Faith Associates, 2009.
Twelve essential practices for a Christian way of life are offered for family and individual exploration: caring for the body, celebrating life, discernment, dying well, eating well, forgiving, keeping Sabbath, managing household life, participating in community, praying, reading the Bible, and transforming the world. Companion booklet for children: *Living Well Children's Workbook: Christian Practices for Children.*

Sexuality Information and Education Council of the United States (SIECUS). *Guidelines for Comprehensive Sexuality Education: Kindergarten—12th grade,* 3rd ed. Washington, DC: National Guidelines Task Force, 2004.
A resource to help educators create new sexuality education programs and evaluate already existing curricula. The guidelines, developed by a national task force of experts in the fields of adolescent development, health care, and education, provide a framework of the key concepts, topics, and messages that all sexuality education programs would ideally include. www.siecus.org/_data/global/images/guidelines.pdf.

University of Pennsylvania. *Making Proud Choices! A Safer Sex Approach to STDs, Teen Pregnancy, and HIV Prevention.* Philadelphia: University of Pennsylvania.
An eight-module curriculum that provides young adolescents with the knowledge, confidence, and skills necessary to reduce their risk of sexually transmitted diseases (STDs), HIV, and pregnancy by abstaining from sex or using condoms if they choose to have sex. It is based on cognitive behavioral theories, focus groups, and the researchers' extensive experience working with youth. The *Making Proud*

Choices! curriculum has four major components. One component focuses on goals and dreams and adolescent sexuality. The second component is knowledge. It covers information about the etiology, transmission, and prevention of STDs, HIV, and teenage pregnancy. The third component focuses on beliefs and attitudes. The fourth component focuses on skills and self-efficacy. It covers negotiation-refusal skills and condom use skills, and provides time for practice, reinforcement, and support. http://recapp.etr.org/Recapp/index.cfm?fuseaction=pages.ebpDetail&PageID=128.

Virginia Theological Seminary. "Relationships: A Guide for Leadership Teams" as part of *The Episcopal Curriculum for Older Youth*. Alexandria, VA: Virginia Theological Seminary, 1997.

Based on the Baptismal Covenant, nine sessions are offered for high school students to study relationships on the following topics: know yourself, getting to know others, costs of relationships, true friendship, romantic love, getting along with family, and respecting others. www.vts.edu/ftpimages/95/download/Relationships%20Guide-Year%201.pdf.

ETHICS

Ellison, Marvin M. *Making Love Just: Sexual Ethics for Perplexing Times*. Minneapolis: Fortress Press, 2012.

Ellison strives to offer a new sexual ethic for the contemporary day. He invites the reader to struggle with sexual issues of today to create a more sexually just society. He poses questions about sex and sexuality in singleness, older adulthood, marriage, divorce, and about sexual orientation and identity. An excellent choice for any leader, family, or congregation interested in being pushed to think deeply about some of the most challenging sexual ethic questions of our day.

Farley, Margaret A. *Just Love: A Framework for Christian Sexual Ethics*. New York: Continuum International Publishing Group, 2006.

A framework for sexual ethics whereby justice is the criterion for all loving, including love related to sexual activity and relationships. It begins with historical and cross-cultural explorations, then addresses the large questions of embodiment, gender, and sexuality, and finally delineates the justice framework for sexual ethics.

Jung, Patricia Beattie and Stephens, Darryl W., Eds. *Professional Sexual Ethics: A Holistic Ministry Approach*. Minneapolis: Fortress Press, 2013.

Sexual health is an essential part of maintaining professional relationships in ministry. Each chapter includes an analysis of common ministry situations, discussion questions, practical guidelines, and resources for further study.

Sedgwick, Timothy F. *The Christian Moral Life: Practices of Piety*. New York: Seabury Books, 2008.

The way of life we call Christian is lived in relationships to others. Christian faith, understood as practical piety, calls for a life opened to the world at large, concerned for the "stranger" as well as for the neighbor. Sedgwick further emphasizes that the Christian life is grounded in the experience and worship of God. His work thus develops Christian ethics as "sacramental ethics," an ethic that has at its center a deepening encounter with God.

THEOLOGY

Ellison, Marvin M. and Kelly Brown Douglas, eds. *Sexuality and the Sacred: Sources for Theological Reflection*, 2nd ed. Louisville: Westminster John Knox Press, 2010.

A collection of essays written about a variety of sexual ethic and theological issues. The second edition offers further conversation on topics from the first edition in addition to offering new insights on the current conversation. An excellent addition to any theological collection.

Gomes, Peter J. *The Good Book: Reading the Bible with Mind and Heart*. San Francisco: HarperSanFrancisco, 1996.

A commonsense and theological analysis of what the Bible means for us today. As an African-American gay man, Gomes reviews the biblical passages on sexuality and race, as well as how the whole Bible can find a place in our emotional and political lives, as well as in our religious beliefs.

Mitchell, Leonel L. *Praying Shapes Believing: A Theological Commentary on The Book of Common Prayer.* Revised edition. Edited by Ruth A. Meyers. New York: Seabury Books, 2016.

Offers a comprehensive explanation of the theology behind the 1979 *Book of Common Prayer*, including its baptismal theology and the Baptismal Covenant.

Nelson, James B. *Body Theology*. Louisville: Westminster John Knox Press, 1992.

Nelson believes sexuality is central to the mystery of human experience and to the human relationship with God. He seeks to identify what scripture and tradition says about sexuality, focusing on three areas of concern: sexual theology, men's issues, and biomedical ethics.

Nelson, James B. *Embodiment: An Approach to Sexuality and Christian Theology*. Minneapolis: Augsburg Publications, 1978.

Embodiment is a classic, foundational resource in the Christian Church for conversation about sexuality. Nelson's book greatly shaped development of Christian sexual ethics and sexual theology the past thirty years. *Embodiment* focuses on Jesus as the word made flesh, Jesus as understanding and embracing human sexuality in its fullest. Nelson explores what "our experience as sexual human beings means for the way in which we understand and attempt to live out the faith" and what it means "that we as body-selves are invited to participate in the reality of God" (page 9). We are created in, by, and for community. Through discussion about desire, the ascetic life, homosexuality, marriage, community, worship, Eucharist, and alienation, Nelson explores ways in which our sexuality enters and shapes our experience of the Christian faith.

Nelson, James B. and Sandra Longfellow, eds. *Sexuality and the Sacred: Sources for Theological Reflection*. Louisville: Westminster John Knox Press, 1994.

While this collection of essays is now twenty years old, they offer great value to today's theological discussion. Along with the 2nd edition, this anthology is a great addition to any theological collection.

Paulsell, Stephanie. *Honoring the Body: Meditations on a Christian Practice*. San Francisco: Jossey-Bass, 2002.

This is one of the best resources available on caring for the body in a holistic way from a Christian perspective. Paulsell lays the foundation of the body and soul as one unit, inseparable, and carries that through to a Christian framework of the incarnation, death, and resurrection of Christ. She shares reflections and insight about all the ways we as individuals, families, and church communities do and should care about the body. This book is an excellent resource for parents, small-group discussion, anyone wanting an easy-to-understand book about the sacredness of the body.

Smith, Christian and Melinda Lundquist Denton. *Soul Searching: The Religious and Spiritual Lives of American Teenagers*. New York: Oxford University Press, 2005.

This book reports the findings of the National Study of Youth and Religion, the largest and most detailed study of its kind ever undertaken. The results show that religion and spirituality are, in fact, significant in the lives of many American teenagers. Among many other discoveries, they find that teenagers are far more influenced by the religious beliefs and practices of their parents and caregivers than commonly thought. This book provides an excellent window into understanding the lives of our teenagers.

Smith, Christian and Patricia Snell. *Souls in Transition: The Religious and Spiritual Lives of Emerging Adults*. New York: Oxford University Press, 2009.

This is the follow-up study to the landmark book, *Soul Searching: The Religious and Spiritual Lives of American Teenagers*. *Souls in Transition* reveals how the religious practices of the teenagers portrayed in *Soul Searching* have grown, lessened, and changed as they have moved into adulthood. The book describes a picture of the cultural world for the emerging young adults, how that culture shapes their religious outlooks, and what the consequences are for religious faith and practice in America more generally.

Whitehead, Evelyn Eaton and James Whitehead. *Wisdom of the Body: Making Sense of our Sexuality*. Spring Valley, NY: The Crossroad Publishing Company, 2001.

The book explores the corporate body of Christians and the Church universal, as the authors believe the communal body has experience and wisdom with respect to the sexuality of Christians. The book focuses on three areas: sexuality, intimacy, and gender. The best feature of the book is the reflective questions and additional resources provided at the end of each chapter, making this a great resource for discussion groups or education classes.

Williams, Rowan D. "The Body's Grace." *Theology and Sexuality: Classic and Contemporary Readings*, edited by Eugene F. Rogers, Jr., 309–321. New Jersey: Blackwell Publishing, 2002.

In this article Williams examines sexuality, marriage, celibacy, and same-sex relationships. While this article is dense, it is worthy of multiple reads. He incorporates scripture as well as other theologians, stresses mutuality and the use of creation and redemption language. He provides a positive understanding of the challenges of the single vocation. This article stresses the examination of the whole story of scripture and culture.

Winner, Lauren F. *Real Sex: The Naked Truth about Chastity*. Grand Rapids: Brazos Press, 2006.

A candid look at single Christians and the difficulty and importance of sexual chastity. Winner grounds her discussion of chastity first and foremost in Scripture. She confronts cultural lies about sex and challenges how we talk about sex in church. She argues that sex is communal rather than private, personal rather than public. Includes discussion questions.

FAITH & HUMAN DEVELOPMENT

Berman, Laura. *Talking to Your Kids About Sex: Turning "The Talk" into a Conversation for Life*. New York: DK Publishing, 2009.

Backed by scientific information, Dr. Berman writes an accessible, practical book designed as a guide to help parents as they communicate their beliefs and family sexual values to their children. She offers discussion questions for parents to discuss with their partners as well as discussion questions to help conversation with one's child. She is neutral on abstinence, sexual orientation, and gender identity. *Talking to Your Kids About Sex* focuses on empowering parents and empowering children in understanding the many facets of sex and decision-making about sex.

Dobbs, David. "Beautiful Brains." *National Geographic,* October 2011.

Dobbs offers an insightful, scientific, fun-to-read article about teenagers and how their brains work. He talks about why teens take chances, explaining how risk/reward is different in the teenaged brain than it is for adults. http://ngm. nationalgeographic.com/2011/10/teenage-brains/dobbs-text.

Dykstra, Robert C., Allan Hugh Cole Jr., and Donald Capps. *Losers, Loners, and Rebels: The Spiritual Struggles of Boys*. Louisville: Westminster John Knox Press, 2007.

Dykstra, Cole, and Capps offer engaging and insightful narratives about their boyhoods. Interwoven with developmental information, the stories are written with the purpose to create remembering one's childhood; they provide no list of practical wisdom for fathers, mothers, teachers, or youth leaders. The authors focus on boyhood between ages 11–14 as painful and lonely; however, it is through the negative experiences of these years that leads to the spiritual growth of adolescent boys. For men and women alike, this resource is an interesting read that offers insight into the inner lives of middle-school-aged boys.

_____. *The Faith and Friendship of Teenage Boys*. Louisville: Westminster John Knox Press, 2012.

This book is a follow-up to the authors' project *Losers, Loners, and Rebels: The Spiritual Struggles of Boys*. This book focuses on friendships between adolescent boys as an expression of faith. The authors acknowledge the importance of male/female friendships, but for their research and writing, focus on the importance of male/male friendships during the adolescent years.

Fowler, James W. and Mary Lynn Dell. "Stages of Faith from Infancy through Adolescence: Reflections of Three Decades of Faith Development Theory." *The Handbook of Spiritual Development in Childhood and Adolescence,* edited by Eugene D. Roehlkepartain, Pamela Ebstyne King, Linda Wagener, and Peter L. Benson, 34–45. London: Sage Publications, 2006.

Fowler's most well-known work, *Stages of Faith,* changed the way modern-day theologians and church educators thought about faith development through the lifespan. Based on the past thirty years of experience, this short article is a great snapshot of the psycho/social/spiritual development of children and youth as we understand it today. A must-read for anyone curious about faith development and for all those who plan educational or worship experiences for children and adolescents.

Keeley, Robert J. "Faith Development and Faith Formation: More Than Just Ages and Stages" in *Lifelong Faith*, Fall 2010, 20–27.

A short, but thorough review of the faith development theories used for children, adolescents, and adults. www.faith formationlearningexchange.net/uploads/5/2/4/6/5246709/faith_development__faith_formation_-_keeley.pdf.

Mercer, Joyce Ann. *GirlTalk/GodTalk: Why Faith Matters to Teenage Girls and Their Parents*. San Francisco: Jossey-Bass, 2008.

An all-around top resource for anyone wanting to better understand the inner lives of adolescent girls. This work brings to light concerns about the intersection of religion, gender, and family relationships in the lives of teenage girls. Mercer provides not only powerful stories from the lives of her interviewees, she weaves in developmental theory and practical advice. Growing up in an over-programed, hypersexualized, noisy world, more than ever girls need a place to have conversation about their life and their faith. *GirlTalk/GodTalk* demonstrates a relational space in which girls could construct their worldview as they spoke about their lives, what matters to them, and where they need more. This work brings to light concerns about the intersection of religion, gender, and family relationships in the lives of teenage girls.

SOCIOLOGY & CULTURE

Bauer, Jill and Ronna Gradus, directors. *Hot Girls Wanted*. Two to Tangle Productions, 2015.

An American documentary available about porn, the Internet, and the girl next door. This Netflix original documentary follows the lives of young 18- to 25-year-old women entering the amateur pornography world. 84 minutes.

Clark, Chap. *Hurt 2.0: Inside the World of Today's Teenagers.* Grand Rapids: Baker Academic, 2011.

A penetrating look into the contemporary adolescent experience including the hurting hearts of today's young people. Topics include stress, abandonment issues, social networking, gaming, promiscuity, self-mutilation, loneliness, and suicide.

Tigert, Leanne McCall and Timothy Brown, eds. *Coming Out Young and Faithful*. Cleveland: Pilgrim Press, 2001.

A powerful collection of writings from youth and adults about their coming-out experiences and their faith.

Valenti, Jessica. *The Purity Myth: How America's Obsession with Virginity Is Hurting Young Women*. Berkeley, CA: Seal Press, 2010.

Through in-depth cultural and social analysis, Valenti reveals that powerful messaging on both extremes—ranging from abstinence curriculum to *Girls Gone Wild* infomercials—place a young woman's worth entirely on her sexuality. *The Purity Myth* presents a revolutionary argument that girls and women are overly valued for their sexuality, as well as solutions for a future without a damaging emphasis on virginity.

SPECIFICALLY FOR PARENTS

Brill, Stephanie and Pepper, Rachel. *The Transgender Child: A Handbook for Families and Professionals*. San Francisco, CA: Cleis Press, Inc., 2008.

A guide for parents of transgender and gender-variant children that seeks to fill a gap in both parenting and transgender literature. Building on existing research, as well as the authors' experiences working with families, the book provides an overview of issues as well as concrete solutions to common problems (for example, recommending that parents role-play answering questions from strangers.) The emphasis is always on love: Parents must navigate a course that will allow them to support and unconditionally love their child. Rather than recommending a single path, the authors acknowledge the different challenges faced by transgender and gender-variant children. The authors recognize that all families must start where they are, but offer practical tools for advocating and parenting.

Harris, Robie. *It's Not the Stork! A Book About Girls, Boys, Babies, Bodies, Families and Friends*. Somerville, MA: Candlewick Press, 2008.

Vetted and approved by science, health, and child development experts, the information is age-appropriate for preschoolers and early elementary-aged children, up-to-date, scientifically accurate, and always aimed at helping kids feel knowledgeable and comfortable about their own bodies, about how they were born, and about the family they are part of.

_____. *It's Perfectly Normal: Changing Bodies, Growing Up, Sex, and Sexual Health*. Somerville: MA, Candlewick Press, 2014.

Part of The Family Library series, this book is written for ages ten and up. Newly updated for its 20th anniversary, *It's Perfectly Normal* includes information on subjects such as safe and savvy Internet use, gender identity, emergency contraception, and more. Providing accurate and up-to-date answers to nearly every imaginable question, *It's Perfectly Normal* is a must-have resource for every household.

_____. *It's So Amazing! A Book about Eggs, Sperm, Birth, Babies, and Families.* Somerville, MA: Candlewick Press, 2014.
　　The second of The Family Library series by Robie Harris provides clear, straightforward answers. Written with the interests of children age seven and up in mind, Harris explains how things work, while giving kids a healthy understanding of their bodies.

King, Zach and King, Kimberly. *I Said No! A Kid-to-Kid Guide to Keeping Private Parts Private*. Weaverville, CA: Boulden Publishing, 2008.
　　A sexual abuse prevention book for kids that helps children set healthy boundaries for their private parts. This topic can be a daunting and awkward task for parents, counselors and educators. Written from a kid's point of view, *I Said No!* makes this task a lot easier. Using a simple, direct, decidedly "non-icky" approach that doesn't dumb down the issues involved, as well as an easy-to-use system to help kids rehearse and remember appropriate responses to help keep them safe. This story was inspired by children and is a wonderful tool for parents as they try to educate their children on the very important topic of sexual abuse prevention. A must-have sexual abuse prevention book for all families and professionals who care for children.

Kitch, Anne E. *Taking the Plunge: Baptism and Parenting*. New York: Morehouse Publishing, 2006.
　　Kitch, a respected Episcopal Church educator and author, writes in a reflective manner with real-life stories. She helps parents explore how the Baptismal Covenant helps to shape

the experience of raising children. This book is as much about raising children as it is about baptism. This is a wonderful educational piece for parents, godparents, and any adult involved in the spiritual life of a child.

Ott, Kate. *Sex + Faith: Talking with Your Child from Birth to Adolescence*. Louisville: Westminster John Knox Press, 2013.
   Sex + Faith helps parents incorporate their faith values with sexual information so they can answer questions, discuss sexuality at each stage of childhood, and show support of sexual differences. Complete with developmental information, biblical and faith stories, and practical questions, this book is an easy-to-use reference guide for parents of kids of all ages.

Sherman, Joanne. *Because It's My Body!* Scotch Plains, NJ: S.A.F.E. for Children Publishing, L.L.C., 2002.
   Focusing on empowerment and prevention, this approachable book gives young children a way to reject unwanted, possibly harmful physical contact by adults and other kids. Its non-confrontational tone relays the importance of saying no without veering into descriptions of molestation—teaching children without scaring them. Diverse illustrations allow young readers to identify with the characters in the book and, without focusing on sexuality, the scenarios show children how to start the process of defining physical boundaries by teaching them that their entire body belongs to them. By giving them the tools to stand up for themselves, parents and educators can set kids on a path to protecting themselves from unwanted touching and abuse.

Wiseman, Rosalind. *Queenbees and Wannabees: Helping Your Daughter Survive Cliques, Gossip, Boyfriends, and the New Realities of Girl World*. New York: Three Rivers Press, 2002.
   Every teacher, mentor, parent, or anyone who works with middle school or high school aged youth should read this book.

FOR CHILDREN WITH LEARNING DIFFERENCES

Champagne, Marilyn P. and Walker-Hirsch, Leslie W. *Circles Curriculum Program*. Santa Barbara, CA: James Stanfield Publishing Company, 2010.

The Circles Program assists students to discriminate different degrees of intimacy and to adapt their behaviors accordingly. The program teaches students how relationships can be formed and maintained according to the social norms of our day. Thus, the Circles Program lays the foundation for people with social deficits due to their disabilities to manage the amount of personal responsibility and social integration in their lives.

_____ and Walker-Hirsch, Leslie W. *Life Horizons Curriculum Program*. Santa Barbara, CA: James Stanfield Publishing Company, 2010.

Life Horizons I addresses the physiological and emotional aspects of being male and female. It is the most widely used sex education program for individuals with developmental and learning disabilities. *Life Horizons II* focuses on attitudes and behaviors that promote good interpersonal relationships and responsible sexual behavior.

Couwenhoven, Terri. *Teaching Children with Down Syndrome about Their Bodies, Boundaries, and Sexuality: A Guide for Parents and Professionals*. Bethesda, MD: Woodbine House, Inc., 2007.

The author combines her experience as a sexuality educator with her experience as the mother of two teenage girls—one of whom has Down syndrome—to present comprehensive information in an engaging and understandable manner. Couwenhoven blends factual information and practical ideas for teaching children with Down syndrome about their bodies, puberty, and sexuality. In an easy-to-read, non-clinical style, the book covers relevant issues and concerns for children of all ages. Each chapter highlights important points with key messages, teaching activities, parental pauses, and anecdotes, all of which prompt readers to stop and consider concepts or values associated with a particular topic. The final chapter covers the special concerns of parents who are now teaching teenage or adult children about sexuality for the first time. It concludes with extensive appendices containing invaluable teaching materials and illustrations of body parts and functions.

Hénault, Isabelle. *Aspergers Syndrome and Sexuality From Adolescence through Adulthood*. Philadelphia: Jessica Kingsley Publishers, 2006.

    In this comprehensive and unique guide, Isabelle Hénault delivers practical information and advice on issues ranging from puberty and sexual development, gender identity disorders, couples' therapy to guidelines for sex education programs and maintaining sexual boundaries. This book will prove indispensable to parents, teachers, counselors, and individuals with Aspergers themselves.

Hartman, Davida. *Sexuality and Relationship Education for Children and Adolescents with Autism Spectrum Disorders: A Professional's Guide to Understanding, Preventing Issues, Supporting Sexuality and Responding to Inappropriate Behaviours*. Philadelphia: Jessica Kingsley Publishers, 2014.

    Offering practical teaching advice geared toward the needs of young people on the autism spectrum this author begins with information on good practice, policy, teaching methods, and recent research. The book then divides into key sex education topics that assist professionals in developing their own individualized and developmentally appropriate curricula. Discussion and activity ideas and reproducible resources including instructional stories, checklists, and illustrations are included. The final section demonstrates how to respond to ongoing patterns of inappropriate behavior and put together a behavior plan.

Schwier, Karin Melberg and Hingsburger, Dave. *Sexuality: Your Sons and Daughters with Intellectual Disabilities*. Baltimore, MD: Paul H. Brookes Publishing Co, 2000.

Experts in their field, Schwier and Hingsburger teach readers how to interact with children—no matter their age or ability—in a way that increases self-esteem, encourages appropriate behavior, empowers them to recognize and respond to abuse, and enables them to develop lifelong relationships. Parents share the joys and challenges of raising a child with an intellectual disability as they offer helpful advice and practical strategies. And you'll hear individuals with intellectual disabilities explain what's important to them.

Vredeveld, Ronald C. *Caring Relationships: Helping People with Mental Impairments Understand God's Gift of Sexuality*. Grand Rapids, MI: CRC Publications, 2001.

Written as a companion piece to *Sexuality: Your Sons and Daughters with Intellectual Disabilities*. This book, along with many of the intellectual disability books, needs to be updated. It is still an excellent starting resource for any congregation wanting to support families and individuals with an intellectual disability.

SEXUAL MISCONDUCT AND AWARENESS TRAINING

Melton, Joy Thornburg Melton. *Safe Sanctuaries: Reducing the Risk of Abuse in the Church for Children and Youth*. Nashville: Discipleship Resources, 2008.

A United Methodist resource designed for congregations to help them develop a safe sanctuary policy for children, youth, and elders in any congregation. This resource helps congregational leadership establish or update a policy broken down into ten steps. Also offers articles and webinars on a variety of specific topics related to Safe Sanctuaries, such as the virtual world, retreats and camps, elder care, and supervising youth events.

Safeguarding God's Children and *Safeguarding God's People*. New York: Church Pension Group with Praesidium.

The Episcopal Church's authorized sexual misconduct prevention training program and model policies. An online or in-person training for adults that helps congregations maintain a safe environment. www.cpg.org/administrators /insurance/preventing-sexual-misconduct/overview/ and www .safeguardingonline.org. As of this publication, an appointed Task Force is working to create new model policies for the protection of children and youth in The Episcopal Church as well as compiling new models and resources for training. These will be reported to the 2018 General Convention.

Stewards of Children. Charleston, SC: Darkness to Light.

This particular program raises awareness of the prevalence and consequences of child sexual abuse by educating adults about the steps they can take to prevent, recognize, and react responsibly to the reality of child sexual abuse. Nationally recognized and used by many organizations, they offer current information on abuse statistics, economic impact, adult responsibility, and prevention. www.d21.org.

GENERAL CONVENTION RESOLUTIONS

RESOLUTION 2009–A161
REQUEST HIV/AIDS PREVENTION IN CHURCH EDUCATION PROGRAMS

Resolved, That the 76th General Convention of The Episcopal Church urges provinces, dioceses, congregations, and worshiping communities to include accurate and comprehensive HIV and AIDS prevention in youth education programs; and be it further

Resolved, That The Episcopal Church encourage its congregations and worshiping communities to offer educational programming to interested parents and grandparents on how to discuss sex with their children; and be it further

Resolved, That the National Episcopal AIDS Coalition (NEAC) and National Episcopal Health Ministries (NEHM) be requested to compile appropriate secular and theological resources for this programming, including but not limited to: abstinence, resisting peer pressure and methods for preventing HIV, other STDs and pregnancy; and be it further

Resolved, That NEHM and NEAC further be requested to make these materials available to clergy, parishes, parish nurses, Christian educators, and Episcopal schools.

General Convention, *Journal of the General Convention of The Episcopal Church, Anaheim, 2009* (New York: General Convention, 2009), 195.

RESOLUTION 2000–A046
URGE CONVERSATION WITH YOUTH
AND YOUNG ADULTS ABOUT SEXUALITY

Resolved, That the 73rd General Convention of The Episcopal Church strongly urge dioceses and congregations to provide a safe, hospitable environment for frank conversation with youth and young adults about human sexuality, to share and teach accurate information, and to promote dialogue, within the context of the Baptismal Covenant; and be it further

Resolved, That The Episcopal Church Center's Ministries with Young People Cluster, in consultation with provincial networks, identify and recommend comprehensive guidelines and resources for these conversations.

General Convention, *Journal of the General Convention of The Episcopal Church, Denver, 2000* (New York: General Convention, 2001), 202.

RESOLUTION 2000–D049
MAKE AVAILABLE RESOURCES ON ABSTINENCE IN
SEXUALITY MATERIALS FOR YOUTH

Resolved, That because The Episcopal Church has agreed to "include emphasis on abstinence" (1997-A047a) in its AIDS prevention ministry and because the surest way to avoid sexually transmitted diseases is not to have sexual intercourse, the Ministries with Young People Office and other appropriate individuals shall be directed to make available, in addition to the Episcopal Guide to Teens for AIDS Prevention (TAP), supplemental materials on abstinence from the many successful abstinence-based prevention programs.

General Convention, *Journal of the General Convention of The Episcopal Church, Denver, 2000* (New York: General Convention, 2001), 653.

RESOLUTION 1997–D032
ACKNOWLEDGE THE CHURCH'S UNIQUE ROLE IN MINISTERING TO YOUTH

Resolved, That this 72nd General Convention, while recognizing that parents are the loving source of authority in the education of children, acknowledge the Church's unique role in ministering to all youth, particularly in the area of faith and morals: and be it further

Resolved, That all parishes are urged to teach and support sexual abstinence, self-respect, resistance to peer pressure and respect to those who say "no" to sex before marriage.

General Convention, *Journal of the General Convention of The Episcopal Church, Philadelphia, 1997* (New York: General Convention, 1998), 277.

RESOLUTION NUMBER: 1994–C026
ADDRESS YOUTH SUICIDE AND CONFLICTS OVER SEXUALITY

Resolved, the House of Deputies concurring, That the members of this Church seriously address the issues of youth suicide and runaway/throwaway youth, especially as these result from conflict over sexuality, sexual identity, and sexual orientation; and be it further

Resolved, That the congregations and dioceses of this Church are strongly encouraged to identify and use as soon as possible educational materials directed to parents which will assist them in understanding their children's sexuality and in caring for their children regardless of whatever their sexuality may be; and be it further

Resolved, That the Department of Education for Mission and Ministry, through the Youth Ministries Office, be directed to prepare educational materials to help youth understand their sexuality; and be it further

Resolved, That the General Convention allocate $15,000.00 for these purposes for the 1995–1997 Triennium, subject to funding in the budget.

General Convention, *Journal of the General Convention of The Episcopal Church, Indianapolis, 1994* (New York: General Convention, 1995), 778.

RESOLUTION 1988–A089
PROMOTE USE OF MATERIALS ON HUMAN SEXUALITY AND ABORTION FOR ALL AGE GROUPS

Resolved, the House of Deputies concurring, That this 69th General Convention call on the Presiding Bishop and the Executive Council to provide and promote the use of materials on human sexuality, birth control, and family planning for all age groups as part of this Church's on-going Christian Education curricula as reflective of God's creation; and be it further

Resolved, That the topic of abortion be included in the Church's education curricula and that these materials be explicit, with a full understanding of the physical, emotional, and spiritual realities and risks involved in abortion; and be it further

Resolved, That we encourage the members of this Church to give strong support to responsible local public and private school programs of education in human sexuality.

General Convention, *Journal of the General Convention of The Episcopal Church, Detroit, 1988* (New York: General Convention, 1989), 687.

RESOLUTION 1982–D071
URGE MEMBERS TO TEACH CHILDREN AN ETHOS THAT COUNTERACTS PORNOGRAPHY

Resolved, the House of Bishops concurring, That the 67th General Convention reaffirms the Church's biblical conviction that human sexuality is a gift of God intended to bless and enrich the whole of life, and urges all priests, educators, and parents to provide an ethos in which children may mature in a healthy and responsible understanding of their sexuality, counteracting the dehumanizing influence of exploitive pornography.

General Convention, *Journal of the General Convention of The Episcopal Church, New Orleans, 1982* (New York: General Convention, 1983), C-154.

RESOLUTION 1982–D076
DEVELOP EDUCATIONAL RESOURCES RELATING TO SEXUALITY AND FAMILY LIFE

Resolved, the House of Bishops concurring, That the Executive Council through its Committee on Education for Mission and Ministry develop educational ways by which the Church can assist its people in their formative years (children through adults) to develop moral and spiritual perspectives in matters relating to sexuality and family life.

General Convention, *Journal of the General Convention of The Episcopal Church, New Orleans, 1982* (New York: General Convention, 1983), C-152.

BIBLIOGRAPHY

Bass, Dorothy C. *Practicing Our Faith: A Way of Life for a Searching People.* San Francisco: John Wiley & Sons, 1997.

Bell, Rob. *Sex God: Exploring the Endless Connections Between Sexuality and Spirituality.* Grand Rapids: Zondervan, 2007.

Berman, Laura. *Talking to Your Kids about Sex: Turning "The Talk" into a Conversation for Life.* New York: DK, 2009.

Clark, Chap. *Hurt 2.0: Inside the World of Today's Teenagers*. Grand Rapids: Baker Academic, 2011.

Copeland, Mychal and D'vorah Rose, editors. *Struggling in Good Faith: LGBTQI Inclusion from 13 American Religious Perspectives.* Woodstock, VT: Skylight Paths Publishing, 2016.

Douglas, Kelly Brown. *What's Faith Got to Do with It? Black Bodies/ Christian Souls.* Maryknoll, NY: Orbis Books, 2005.

Dykstra, Robert. *Losers, Loners, and Rebels: The Spiritual Struggles of Boys*. Louisville: Westminster John Knox Press, 2007.

____. *The Faith and Friendship of Teenage Boys*. Westminster John Knox Press, 2012.

Ellison, Marvin M. *Making Love Just: Sexual Ethics for Perplexing Times.* Minneapolis, MN: Fortress Press, 2012.

Ellison, Marvin M. and Kelly Brown Douglas, editors. *Sexuality and the Sacred: Sources for Theological Reflection.* Louisville: Westminster John Knox Press, 2010.

Farley, Margaret. *Just Love: A Framework for Christian Sexual Ethics.* New York: Continuum, 2006.

Fowler, James and Mary Lynne Dell. *Stages of Faith from Infancy through Adolescence: Reflections on Three Decades of Faith*

Development Theory. Thousand Oaks, CA: Sage Publications, 2006.

Hall, Gary R. and Ruth A. Meyers, editors. *Christian Holiness & Human Sexuality: A Study Guide for Episcopalians.* New York: Church Publishing, 2011.

Harris, Robie. *It's Not the Stork! A Book About Girls, Boys, Babies, Bodies, Families and Friends* (The Family Library). Candlewick, 2008.

____. *It's Perfectly Normal: Changing Bodies, Growing Up, Sex, and Sexual Health* (The Family Library). Candlewick, 2014.

____. *It's So Amazing! A Book about Eggs, Sperm, Birth, Babies, and Families* (The Family Library). Candlewick, 2014.

Johnson, Jay Emerson. *Peculiar Faith: Queer Theology for Christian Witness.* New York: Seabury, 2014.

Jung, Patricia Beattie and Stephens, Darryl W., eds. *Professional Sexual Ethics: A Holistic Ministry Approach.* Minneapolis, MN: Fortress Press, 2013.

Kimball, Lisa. "Human Sexuality: Teenagers and the Church." *Resource Book for Ministries with Youth & Young Adults in The Episcopal Church,* edited by Sheryl A. Kujawa and Lois Sibley. New York: The Domestic and Foreign Missionary Society, 1995.

Kitch, Anne E. *Taking the Plunge: Baptism and Parenting.* New York: Morehouse, 2006.

Liturgical Resources 1: I Will Bless You and You Will Be a Blessing, revised and expanded. New York: Church Publishing, 2015.

Mercer, Joyce Ann. *GirlTalk/GodTalk: Why Faith Matters to Teenage Girls—and Their Parents.* San Francisco: Jossey-Bass, 2008.

Nelson, James B. *Embodiment: An Approach to Sexuality and Christian Theology.* Minneapolis: Augsburg, 1978.

Nikkah, John. *Our Boys Speak: Adolescent Boys Write about Their Inner Lives.* New York: St. Martin's Press, 2000.

Noddings, Nel. "The Aims of Education," in *The Curriculum Studies Reader: Second Edition*, edited by David J. Flinders and Stephen J. Thornton. New York: RoutledgeFalmer, 2004.

Ott, Kate. *Sex + Faith: Talking with Your Child from Birth to Adolescence.* Louisville, KY: Westminster John Knox Press, 2013.

Palmer, Parker J. *Let Your Life Speak: Listening for the Voice of Vocation.* San Francisco: Jossey-Bass, 1999.

Paulsell, Stephanie. *Honoring the Body: Meditations on a Christian Practice*. San Francisco: Jossey-Bass, 2002.

Rohr, Richard. *Falling Upward: A Spirituality for the Two Halves of Life.* San Francisco: Jossey-Bass, 2011.

Sedgwick, Timothy F. *The Christian Moral Life: Practices of Piety.* New York: Seabury, 2008.

____. *Sex, Moral Teaching, & the Unity of the Church: A Study of The Episcopal Church*. New York: Morehouse, 2014.

Shandler, Sara. *Ophelia Speaks: Adolescent Girls Write About Their Search for Self*. New York: HarperPerennial, 1999.

Smith, Christian and Melinda Lundquist Denton. *Soul Searching: The Religious and Spiritual Lives of American Teenagers.* New York: Oxford University Press, 2005.

Valenti, Jessica. *The Purity Myth: How America's Obsession with Virginity Is Hurting American Young Women.* Berkeley, CA: Seal Press, 2009.

Virginia Theological Seminary. "Relationships: A Guide for Leadership Teams," *Episcopal Curriculum for Youth*. Alexandria, VA: Virginia Theological Seminary, 1997. No longer in publication, but available for download: www.vts.edu/ftpimages/95/download/Relationships%20Guide-Year%201.pdf.

Williams, Rowan D. "The Body's Grace." *In Theology and Sexuality: Classic and Contemporary Readings*, edited by Eugene F. Rogers, Jr. New Jersey: Blackwell Publishing, 2002.

ACKNOWLEDGMENTS

Thank you to my cowriter Jenny and editor Sharon Pearson for your tireless support, cheerleading, and assistance in writing and editing. Thank you for continuing to push me to do more and to be better. You have taught me so much about writing, faith, and friendship. I am so glad to have partnered with you and developed wonderful friendships during this process.

Thank you to my mentor Henry for your endless support from my master's program to professional church education to finding a voice as a Doctor of Educational Ministry. I would not have been able to do this project without your guidance.

To Hanley, my brother and conversation partner, thank you for your deep, meaningful insights that shaped much of my writing. I greatly appreciate the time, learning, and pictures of yaks while yakking.

To Loren, for your patience in living with my book mess and being unendingly supportive by listening and reading often.

Last, to my family for believing in me, unwaveringly, and for taking such a large interest in this work.

Leslie Choplin

When I reflect on the origins of books about sexuality and faith for The Episcopal Church, I am humbled by the witness and teaching of those who have done work in this area for decades. I am grateful for both their wisdom and legacy. This book grows from the fount of their gifts and discipleship.

Writing a book is a journey and this journey has been shared with Leslie Choplin, who brought a sense of adventure and expertise to our work, and Sharon Pearson, an editor of the first order. Thank you.

For the call to teaching and learning about sexuality, I am grateful to Joann Stratton Tate. For the gift of a sounding board, example, inspiration, and friendship, I am in debt to Betsy Zarzour and Stacy Holley, who share a passion for this work.

If our closest relationships are the incubators and green houses for the Christian life, then my family has been the best spiritual directors. I am profoundly grateful to Katherine, Jonathan, Ben, and Michael, who by their steadfast love have given me the best lessons of all.

Jenny Beaumont

INDEX

NOTES

1   Richard Rohr's Daily Meditation "How to Stay Open," Friday, August 8, 2014 http://myemail
    .constantcontact.com/Richard-Rohr-s-Meditation--How-to-Stay-Open.html?soid=1103098668616&aid=j
    c5Q93T6Yu8
2   Romans 8:38.
3   Education for Mission & Ministry Unit. *Sexuality: A Divine Gift* (New York: The Domestic and Foreign
    Missionary Society, 1987), vii.
4   Lisa Kimball. "Human Sexuality: Teenagers and the Church." *Resource Book for Ministries with Youth
    & Young Adults* ed. Sheryl A. Kujawa and Lois Sibley (New York: The Domestic and Foreign Missionary
    Society, 1995), 102.
5   Rowan D. Williams. "The Body's Grace" in *Theology and Sexuality: Classic and Contemporary Readings*,
    ed. Eugene F. Rogers, Jr. (New Jersey: Blackwell Publishing, 2002), 311–312.
6   Genesis 1:26–27, 31.
7   Gordon D. Kaufman. *God, Mystery, Diversity: Christian Theology in a Pluralistic World*. (Minneapolis:
    Augsburg Fortress, 1996), 97.
8   *Liturgical Resources 1: I Will Bless You and You Will Be a Blessing* (New York: Church Publishing, 2015), 39.
9   BCP, 422.
10 *Liturgical Resources 1*, 141.
11 Ibid., 157.
12 Ibid., 42.
13 Luke 10:33–36.
14 Timothy F. Sedgwick. *The Christian Moral Life: Practices of Piety* (New York: NY Seabury Books, 2008), 20.
15 A sermon preached on October 16, 2010 at St. Christopher's Episcopal Church, Grand Blanc, Michigan.
    http://archive.episcopalchurch.org/78703_125526_ENG_HTM.htm.
16 For more on idolatry see *The Christian Moral Life*, 63–69.
17 Luke 10:27.
18 *Sexuality: A Divine Gift*, 4.
19 Sedgwick. *Sex, Moral Teaching, & the Unity of the Church*, 9.
20 BCP, 336.
21 Sedgwick. *The Christian Moral Life*, 32.
22 Romans 12:2.
23 John 1:14.
24 Anne E. Kitch. *Taking the Plunge: Baptism and Parenting* (New York: Morehouse Publishing, 2006), xiv.
25 Kitch, 39.
26 Mitchell, 102.
27 Nelson, 30.
28 2012 General Convention resolution (A049) to Authorize Liturgical Resources for Blessing Same-Sex
    Relationships: www.episcopalarchives.org/cgi-bin/acts/acts_resolution.pl?resolution=2012-A049.
29 General Convention approves marriage equality. http://episcopaldigitalnetwork.com/ens/2015/07/01/
    general-convention-approves-marriage-equality/.

30 Cameron Partridge. "The Episcopal Church." *Struggling in Good Faith: LGBTQI Inclusion from 13 American Religious Perspectives,* ed. Mychal Copeland and D'vorah Rose (Woodstock, VT: Skylight Paths Publishing, 2016) (on Kindle).

31 *Liturgical Resources 1,* 44.

32 Jay Emerson Johnson. *Peculiar Faith: Queer Theology for Christian Witness* (New York: Seabury, 2014), 234.

33 Williams, 317.

34 William Countryman. *The Archbishops in Secret*, January 19, 2016. "Bill Countryman Talks About . . ." www.billcountryman.com/?p=294 (accessed January 23, 2016).

35 Robert C. Dykstra, Allan Hugh Cole Jr., Donald Capps. *Losers, Loners, and Rebels: The Spiritual Struggles of Boys* (Louisville: Westminster John Knox Press, 2007), 86.

36 Dykstra, 56–57.

37 Williams, 11–12.

38 Leonel L. Mitchell. *Praying Shapes Believing: A Theological Commentary on The Book of Common Prayer* (Harrisonburg, PA: Morehouse Publishing, 1985), 99.

39 Stephanie Paulsell. *Honoring the Body: Meditations on a Christian Practice* (San Francisco: Jossey-Bass, 2002), 7–8.

40 Paulsell, 17, and Margaret Farley. *Just Love: A Framework for Christian Sexual Ethics* (New York: The Continuum International Publishing Group, Inc., 2006), 115–116.

41 Richard Rohr's Daily Meditation "How to Stay Open."

42 Paulsell, xiv.

43 Karen Lebacqz. "Appropriate Vulnerability: A Sexual Ethic for Singles," in *Sexuality and the Sacred: Sources for Theological Reflection,* ed. Marvin M. Ellison and Kelly Brown Douglas (Louisville: Westminster John Knox Press, 2010), 272–273.

44 Paulsell, 152.

45 Ibid., 157.

46 Ibid., 9.

47 James B. Nelson *Embodiment: An Approach to Sexuality and Christian Theology* (Minneapolis, MN: Augsburg Publications, 1978), 29.

48 Dykstra, 86.

49 www.pewforum.org/2015/11/03/u-s-public-becoming-less-religious/.

50 Christian Smith and Melinda Lundquist Denton. *Soul Searching: The Religious and Spiritual Lives of American Teenagers* (New York: Oxford University Press, 2005), 39.

51 Joyce Ann Mercer. *GirlTalk/GodTalk: Why Faith Matters to Teenage Girls—and Their Parents* (San Francisco: Jossey-Bass, 2008), 127.

52 YMCA of the USA, Dartmouth Medical School, and Institute for American Values, *Hardwired to Connect: The New Scientific Case for Authoritative Communities* (New York: Institute for American Values, 2003), 27.

53 Kitch, xiv.

54 Paulsell, 154.

55 Ibid., 126.

56 John 16:13.

57 www.lacigreen.tv/#!about/c1ro4.

58 www.ted.com/talks/al_vernacchio_sex_needs_a_new_metaphor_here_s_one?language=en.

59 WHO, 2006a www.who.int/topics/sexual_health/en/.

60 Luke 23:32–43.

61 Matthew 26:36–46.

62 Matthew 21:12–13.

63 Paulsell, 8.

64 Sedgwick, *A Christian Moral Life*, 55.

65 *Sexuality: A Divine Gift*, 6.

66 Ibid.

67 The original image of the Genderbread Person was created and copyrighted in 2005 by Christina Gonzalez, Vanessa Prell, Jack Rivias, Jarrod Schwartz for *Just Communities Central Coast* of Santa Barbara, California. A number of other "genderbread" figures have since been designed, without the permission of the original creators. We have chosen to use this original image in *These Are Our Bodies*. Used with permission.

68 Language Justice Initiative. *Social Justice Glossary of Terms* (Santa Barbara, CA: Just Communities, 2014). http://media.wix.com/ugd/53f282_e48ea44e7a144cbdab6831961616fffa.pdf (accessed January 17, 2016).

69 www.transstudent.org/gender (accessed January 25, 2016).

70 *Answers to Your Questions: For a Better Understanding of Sexual Orientation & Homosexuality* (Washington, DC: American Psychological Association, 2008) www.apa.org/topics/lgbt/orientation.pdf (accessed January 17, 2016).

71 For more information, download *Peeing In Peace: A Resource Guide for Transgender Activists and Allies* (San Francisco: Transgender Law Center, 2005). http://transgenderlawcenter.org/issues/public-accomodations/peeing-in-peace (accessed January 26, 2016).

72 Ellison, 141–142.

73 Partridge (Kindle edition).

74 Paulsell, 152.

75 www.health.harvard.edu/blog/regular-exercise-changes-brain-improve-memory-thinking-skills-201404097110.

76 https://sleepfoundation.org/ask-the-expert/electronics-the-bedroom (accessed January 6, 2016).

77 https://sleepfoundation.org/ask-the-expert/sleep-hygiene (accessed January 6, 2016).

78 Mark 1:32–39.

79 Sedgwick. *The Christian Moral Life*, 30.

80 John Roberto. "Caring for the Body" in *Living Well: Christian Practices for Everyday Life* (Naugatuck, CT: Lifelong Faith Associates, 2009), 1–9.

81 www.dove.us/social-mission/campaign-for-real-beauty.aspx (accessed January 6, 2016).

82 www.bbc.com/news/world-europe-35130792 (accessed February 4, 2016).

83 www.anad.org/get-information/about-eating-disorders/eating-disorders-statistics/ (accessed February 4, 2016).

84 1 Corinthians 6:19–20.

85 The Mazzoni Center. *Code of Conduct* (2015). www.mazzonicenter.org (accessed January 24, 2016).

86 http://www.search-institute.org/research/developmental-relationships/families (accessed January 6, 2016).

87 Kent Pekel, Eugene C. Roehlkepartain, Amy K. Syvertsen, and Peter C. Scales. Don't Forget the Families: The Missing Piece in America's Effort to Help All Children Succeed (Minneapolis: Search Institute, 2015) www.search-institute.org/research/developmental-relationships/families and www.search-institute.org/downloadable/SearchInstitute-DontForgetFamilies-Media-Report-10-13-2015.pdf (accessed January 6, 2016).

88 John 10:14.

89 Luke 15:8.

90 *Sexuality: A Divine Gift*, 5.

91 Paulsell, 22.

92 www.faithtrustinstitute.org/blog/marie-fortune/219 (accessed January 6, 2015).

93 Ellison, Marvin M. *Making Love Just: Sexual Ethics for Perplexing Times* (Minneapolis, MN: Fortress Press, 2012), 16.

94 Ibid., 89.

95 Ibid., 90.

96 Ibid., 95.

97 Paulsell, 154.

98 Jessica Valenti. *The Purity Myth: How America's Obsession with Virginity Is Hurting Young Women* (Berkeley, CA: Seal Press, 2010), 23–24.

99 Valenti, 105–106.

100   Valenti, 58.

101   www.barna.org/research/culture-media/research-release/what-americans-believe-about-sex#.
VqezYhEjknQ (accessed January 16, 2016).

102   Richard Rohr's Meditation: "Letting Go as a Way of Life," Center for Action and Contemplation, Sunday,
June 7, 2015. http://myemail.constantcontact.com/Richard-Rohr-s-Meditation--Letting-Go-as-a-Way-of-
Life.html?soid=1103098668616&aid=q5sGX-gQW0I (accessed January 6, 2016).

103   Bell, Rob. *Sex God: Exploring the Endless Connections Between Sexuality and Spirituality* (Grand Rapids:
Zondervan, 2007), 13.

104   Bell, 15.

105   *Sexuality: A Divine Gift*, 9.

106   www.pewforum.org/2015/11/03/u-s-public-becoming-less-religious/.

107   www.nytimes.com/2013/11/26/health/families.html (accessed January 6, 2016).

108   *Moving Toward Full Inclusion: Sexual Orientation and Gender Identity in The United Church of Canada*,
2nd edition. (Toronto: The United Church of Canada, 2014), 52.

109   www.mazzonicenter.org (accessed January 24, 2016).

110   www.glaad.org/sites/default/files/allys-guide-to-terminology_1.pdf.

111   "Student Reports of Bullying and Cyber-Bullying." National Center for Education Statistics and Bureau of
Justice Statistics, School Crime Supplement, 2011 http://nces.ed.gov/pubs2013/2013329.pdf (accessed
January 19, 2016).

112   Matthew 7:3–5.

113   http://episcopaldigitalnetwork.com/ens/2015/01/26/presiding-bishop-preaches-at-st-georges-in-
jerusalem (accessed January 17, 2016).

114   *ThinkB4YouSpeak Educator's Guide: For Discussing and Addressing Anti-Gay Language Among Teens*
(San Francisco: Gay, Lesbian and Straight Education Network, 2008), 22.

115   http://student.bmj.com/student/view-article.html?id=sbmj.e688 (accessed January 17, 2016).

116   www.benrose.org/Resources/article-stds-older-adults.cfm (accessed March 24, 2016).

117   www.episcopalchurch.org/files/downloads/episcopal_congregations_overview_2014_1.pdf (accessed
January 19, 2016).

118   Ellison, 10.

119   *Sexuality: A Divine Gift*, 6.

120   Ellison, 41–58.

121   Paulsell, 165–180.

122   Richard Rohr. *Falling Upward: A Spirituality for the Two Halves of Life* (San Francisco: Jossey-Bass, 2011), 8–9.

123   Parker J. Palmer. *Let Your Life Speak: Listening for the Voice of Vocation* (San Francisco: Jossey-Bass,
1999), 6–7.

124   Sedgwick. *The Christian Moral Life*, 141.

125   Brené Brown. *Daring Greatly: How the Courage to Be Vulnerable Transforms the Way We Live, Love,
Parent, and Lead* (New York: Avery, 2012), 69.

126   Laura E. Berk. *Child Development, 7/e* (Boston: Allyn & Bacon, 2006), 38.

127   Myers, David G. *Myers's Psychology for AP, 2011,* 330–331.

128   David G. Myers. *Myers's Psychology for AP* (New York, Worth Publishers, 2011), 411.

129   Piaget, Jean. *Memory and Intelligence* (London: Routledge and Kegan Paul, 1973).

130   Ross D. Parke and Mary Gauvain. *Child Psychology: A Contemporary Viewpoint, 7th Edition* (Boston:
McGraw Hill Companies, 2008), 278.

131   Myers, 420.

132   Ibid., 424.

133   L. S. Vygotsky. *Mind in Society: The Development of Higher Psychological Processes*. (Cambridge, MA:
Harvard University Press, 1978), 86.

134   Laura E. Berk. *Development Through the Lifespan*, 4th ed. (Boston: Pearson, 2007), 23–24.

135   Lev Vygotsky. "The Problem of the Cultural Development of the Child." 1929.

136   Myers, 425.

137   Albert Bandura. "Observational Learning" in *Learning and Memory,* 2nd edition, ed. John H. Byrne (New
York: Macmillan Reference USA, 2004), 482–484.

138 Myers, 425.
139 Ibid., 451.
140 Berk, *Child Development,*18.
141 Ibid.
142 Erik Erikson. *Identity and the Life Cycle* (New York: International Universities, 1959), 82.
143 Myers, 450.
144 YMCA of the USA, 32.
145 Ibid., 25–26.
146 Ibid., 22.
147 Marvin M. Ellison "Reimagining Good Sex: The Eroticizing of Mutual Respect and Pleasure," in *Sexuality and the Sacred: Sources for Theological Reflection,* ed. Marvin M. Ellison and Kelly Brown Douglas (Louisville, KY: Westminster John Knox Press, 2010), 246.
148 Myers, 449.
149 Ibid., 449.
150 Lapsley, Daniel and Narvaez, Darcia. *Moral Psychology at the Crossroads in Character Psychology and Character Education* (University of Notre Dame Press, 2005), 18.
151 Ibid., 28.
152 Ibid., 32.
153 Marvin W. Berkowitz and John H. Grych. "Fostering Goodness: Teaching Parents to Facilitate Children's Moral Development." *Journal of Moral Education,* Volume 27, Issue 3 (1998), 372. http://parenthood.library.wisc.edu/Berkowitz/Berkowitz.html (accessed January 19, 2016), 372.
154 Ibid., 372.
155 Ibid., 371–391.
156 Ibid., 372.
157 Myers, G-1.
158 Berkowitz and Grych, 374.
159 G. Kochanska, K. Murray, and K.C. Coy (1997). "Inhibitory Control as a Contributor to Conscience in Childhood: From Toddler to School Age." *Child Development 68*, 264.
160 Berkowitz and Grych, 377.
161 Matthew 22:36–40.
162 Berkowitz and Grych, 377.
163 Ibid., 377.
164 G. Kochanska, K. DeVet, M. Goldman, K. Murray, and S. Putnam. (1994). "Maternal Reports of Conscience Development and Temperament in Young Children." *Child Development 65*, 852–868 and G. Kochanska, L. Kuczynski, and M. Radke-Yarrow. (1989). "Correspondence Between Mother's Self-Reported and Observed Child-rearing Practices." *Child Development 60*, 56–63.
165 Berkowitz and Grych, 377.
166 Ibid., 387.
167 Ibid., 394.
168 Ibid., 394–397.
169 Nancy Eisenberg and Paul H. Mussen. *The Roots of Prosocial Behavior in Children* (New York: Cambridge University Press, 1989), 151.
170 Berkowitz and Grych, 371–391.
171 Greg Miller. "Chimps Lend a Hand." *Science* Vol. 311, No. 5765 (March 2, 2006), 1,301–1,303. www.sciencemag.org/news/2006/03/chimps-lend-hand (accessed January 19, 2016).
172 Rebecca Clay. "Helping Kids Care." *Monitor on Psychology* Vol. 37, No. 11 (December 2006), 42.
173 For more information on Fowler's stages of faith see Robert J. Keeley, "Faith Development and Faith Formation: More Than Just Ages and Stages" in *Lifelong Faith* (Naugatuck, CT: Lifelong Faith Associations) Fall 2010 Issue, 20–27. www.faithformationlearningexchange.net/uploads/5/2/4/6/5246709/faith_development__faith_formation_-_keeley.pdf (accessed January 10, 2016).
174 John H. Westerhoff III. *Will Our Children Have Faith?* 3rd revised edition (New York: Morehouse, 2012), 90–98.
175 Westerhoff, *Will Our Children Have Faith?,* 102–105.

176   Berk, *Child Development*, 4–5.

177   Ibid., 5.

178   Ibid., 6.

179   Reaching out physically to people around them is a part of connection with others. Being connected to others is a spiritual action.

180   Steven P. Shelov and Dr. Tanya Altmann. *Caring for Your Baby and Young Child: Birth to Age 5*, 6th ed. (New York: Bantam Books, 2014), 201–365.

181   Henri J. M. Nouwen. "The Healing Touch." *Bread for the Journey* Devotion, March 25, 2015. http://lifetogether.oldcatholic.us/bread0325/ (accessed January 17, 2016).

182   Shelov and Altmann, 337–402.

183   Resources on this topic can be found on pages 253–55.

184   Shelov and Altmann, 407.

185   Rachel A. Ozretich and Sally R. Bowman. *Middle Childhood and Adolescent Development* (Corvallis: OR: Oregon State University, 2001). http://extension.oregonstate.edu/tillamook/sites/default/files/documents/4h/ecno1527.pdf (accessed January 18, 2016).

186   Berk, *Child Development*, 6.

187   Ibid., 203.

188   Laura E. Berk. *Child Development,* 9/e (New York: Pearson, 2012), 203.

189   Ibid., 204.

190   Berk, *Child Development*, 6.

191   A fairness rule is a set of standards that a growing child or adult uses as a measuring tool to gauge their actions and the actions of others to determine whether the action is fair to all those involved. "That is not fair" is a common outcry on playgrounds. Later development emphasizes justice rather than fairness or sameness or equality. Individuals can progress to a later stage. This is characterized by an understanding of justice that is not necessarily providing equal assess or support to all people. Justice includes an understanding that equality of resources leaves many people without the support that they need. Justice and just actions seek righteousness, rather than correctness. Parents may seek to treat their children not with fairness or with equality. Children see this when parents provide more attention to a child who is ill. The treatment is not the same, yet it is just.

192   Ellison, *Making Love Just*, 124.

193   Berman, 6.

194   Centers for Disease Control and Prevention. *Sexually Transmitted Disease Surveillance 2013* (Atlanta: U.S. Department of Health and Human Services, 2014), 58. www.cdc.gov/std/stats13/surv2013-print.pdf (accessed January 17, 2016).

195   www.plannedparenthood.org/about-us/newsroom/press-releases/half-all-teens-feel-uncomfortable-talking-their-parents-about-sex-while-only-19-percent-parents (accessed January 17, 2016).

196   Cheryl B. Aspya, Sara K. Vesely, Roy F. Oman, Sharon Rodine, LaDonna Marshall, and Ken McLeroy "Parental Communication and Youth Sexual Behaviour." *Journal of Adolescence* 30 (2007), 449–466.

197   www.researchgate.net/profile/Kenneth_Mcleroy/publication/7033215_Parental_communication_and_youth_sexual_behaviour/links/02bfe51013d03815ea000000.pdf.;   www.researchgate.net/publication/6960813_Youth-parent_communication_and_youth_sexual_behavior_implications_for_physicians; and http://digitalcommons.unl.edu/cgi/viewcontent.cgi?article=1029&context=commstuddiss   (accessed January 17, 2016).

198   Noddings, Nel. "The Aims of Education." *The Curriculum Studies Reader: Second Edition.* ed. David J. Flinders and Stephen J. Thornton (London: Routledge, 2004), 331–344.

199   Ellison, *Reimagining Good Sex*, 248.

200   Daniel R. Heischman. "Transgender People and Episcopal Schools: An Invitation to Discernment" (National Association of Episcopal Schools, February 2016). www.episcopalschools.org/news/network-member-newsletter/network-archives/articles/transgender-people-and-episcopal-schools-an-invitation-to-discernment. (accessed February 3, 2016).

201   https://uwm.edu/lgbtrc/support/gender-pronouns/ (accessed February 4, 2016).

202   Ibid.

203 *Model District Policy on Transgender and Gender Nonconforming Students* (Gay, Lesbian & Straight Education Network, September 2015). www.glsen.org/article/model-laws-policies (accessed January 25, 2016).

204 www.huffingtonpost.com/2015/02/10/lgbt-adults-self-esteem-study-_n_6654072.html (accessed February 5, 2016).

205 Heischman "Transgender People and Episcopal Schools."

206 www.pflagnyc.org/safeschools (accessed January 25, 2016).

207 Carla Robinson, Voice of Witness: Out of the Box, IntegrityUSA 2012. http://blog.transepiscopal.com/p/out-of-box.html (accessed February 3, 2016).

208 Farley, 34.

209 Toya Richards Hill, "Lecturer Says Blues Can Be a Sacred Discourse Toward Positive View of Sexuality." Louisville Seminary, April 1, 2009. www.lpts.edu/news/2009/04/01/lecturer-says-blues-can-be-a-sacred-discourse-toward-positive-view-of-sexuality (accessed January 8, 2016).

210 Farley, 13.

211 Romans 8:37–39.

212 "Regardless of the extent to which healthy births are affected by teen childbearing vs. other sources of disadvantage in their lives, it is important to understand that, on average, teen mothers and their infant children are at higher risk for preterm delivery, low birth weight, and infant mortality, compared to mothers who postpone childbearing beyond the teen years." Kelleen Kaye. *Why It Matters: Childbearing and Infant Health, The National Campaign to Prevent Teen and Unplanned Pregnancies*. October 2012, 4–5. http://thenationalcampaign.org/sites/default/files/resource-primary-download/childbearing-infant-health.pdf and http://www.capefearteen.org/cfthc.php?section=statistics. This is a readable summary of the data from the National Campaign to Prevent Teen and Unplanned Pregnancy.

213 John 13:34.

214 Ephesians 4:1–6.

215 Richard Rohr. *Immortal Diamond: The Search for Our True Self* (San Francisco: Jossey-Bass, 2013), 3.

216 Brown, 8.

217 *Sexuality: A Divine Gift*, vii.

218 https://www.plannedparenthood.org/learn/sexual-orientation-gender/female-male-intersex (accessed March 28, 2016).

219 WHO, 2006a www.who.int/topics/sexual_health/en/.